Looking for a
PLACE

CURATED BY ROSA MARTÍNEZ

The Third International
SITE Santa Fe Biennial
Santa Fe, New Mexico
July 10 – December 31, 1999

"...THE TIME OF LIFE IS SHORT!

...AND IF WE LIVE, WE LIVE TO TREAD ON KINGS..."

— WILLIAM SHAKESPEARE, *HENRY IV*, ACT 5, SCENE 2

This catalogue was published on the occasion of SITE Santa Fe's
Third International Biennial exhibition *Looking for a Place*,
July 10–December 31, 1999.

SITE Santa Fe dedicates this catalogue to the memory of Jodi Carson.

Grateful acknowledgment is made to the following for their permission to reprint
from previously published material:

Helena Almeida: Text published in conjunction with a show of the artist's work
in 1979 at the Sociedade Nacional de Belas-Artes, Lisbon, Portugal. Reprinted by
permission of the artist.

Louise Bourgeois: Excerpt from "On Cells," included in the exhibition catalogue
for the *Carnegie International, 1991/1992*, The Carnegie Museum of Art, Pittsburgh,
Pennsylvania, 1991. Reprinted by permission of the artist.

Lygia Clark: "We Are the Proposers," poem from *Livro-obra*, a collection of the
artist's writings, 1983. Reprinted by permission of The Clark Family Collection,
Rio de Janeiro, Brazil.

Arthur C. Danto: Excerpt from "Pas de Deux, en Masse," an article on Shirin Neshat in
The Nation, June 28, 1999. Reprinted by permission of the author and *The Nation*.

Barry Lopez: "Directions" from *Desert Notes*, Avon Press, 1976. Reprinted by
permission of Sterling Lord Literistic, Inc. © Barry Holstun Lopez.

Gabriel Orozco: Excerpts from an interview with Benjamin Buchloh included in
the exhibition catalogue for *Clinton is Innocent*, 1998, Musée d'art moderne de la
ville de Paris, Paris, France. Reprinted by permission of Benjamin Buchloh and
Gabriel Orozco.

Theodora Vischer: Excerpts from the essay "New World," included in the exhibition
catalogue for *New World*, 1998–99, Moderna Museet, Stockholm, Sweden, and Museum
für Gegenwartskunst, Basel, Switzerland. Reprinted by permission of the author and
the Moderna Museet, Stockholm.

Editor: Sarah S. King
Associate Editor: Rebecca Friedman
Designer: Bethany Johns Design, New York

Assistant to the curator in Barcelona: María José Balcells

ISBN 0965058395
Library of Congress Card Number: 00–108532

cover:
Yolanda Gutiérrez, *The river whispers
to us, and the snake hisses*, 1999
Photo: Jennifer Esperanza

pages 2–3:
Greenpeace, *Action against the
nuclear-powered aircraft carrier
U.S.S. Eisenhower*, Palma de Mallorca,
Spain, 1998
Photo: Greenpeace/Gremo

DIRECTIONS

FROM **DESERT NOTES** BY BARRY LOPEZ

I would like to tell you how to get there so that you may see all this for yourself. But first a warning: you may already have come across a set of detailed instructions, a map with every bush and stone clearly marked, the meandering courses of dry rivers and other geographical features noted, with dotted lines put down to represent the very faintest of trails. Perhaps there were also warnings printed in tiny red letters along the margins, about the lack of water, the strength of the wind and the swiftness of the rattlesnakes.

Your confidence in these finely etched maps is understandable, for at first glance they seem excellent, the best a man is capable of; but your confidence is misplaced. Throw them out. They are

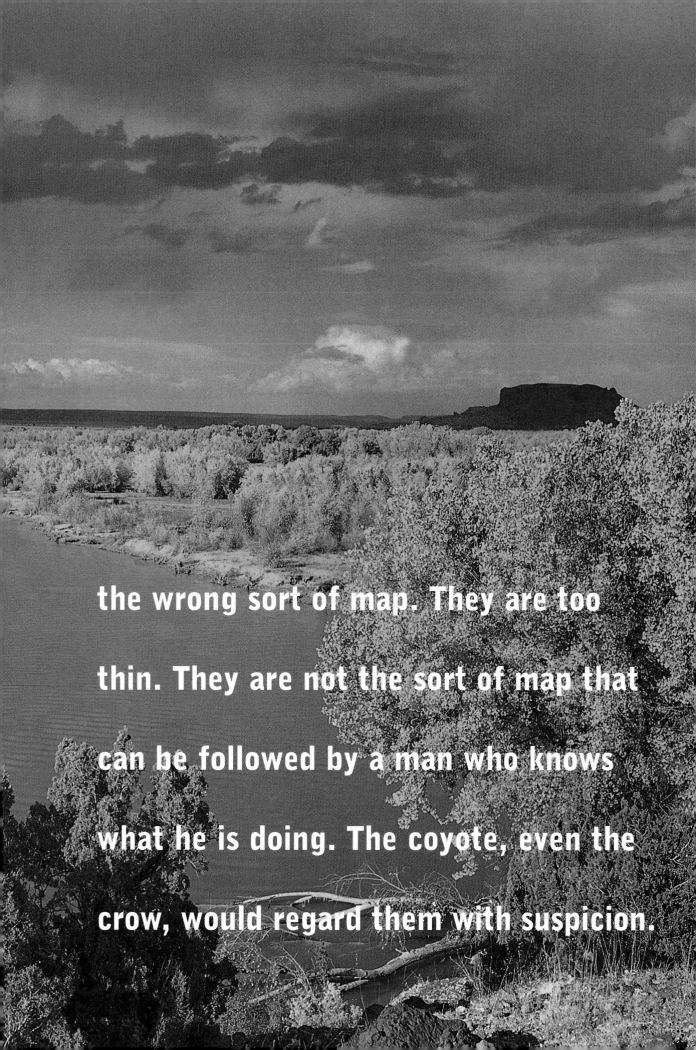

the wrong sort of map. They are too thin. They are not the sort of map that can be followed by a man who knows what he is doing. The coyote, even the crow, would regard them with suspicion.

There is, I should warn you, doubt too about the directions I will give you here, but they are the very best that can be had. They will not be easy to follow. Where it says left you must go right sometimes. Read south for north sometimes. It depends a little on where you are coming from, but not entirely.

I am saying you will have doubts.

If you do the best you can you will have no trouble.

(When you get there you may wish to make up a map for yourself for future reference. It is the only map you will ever trust. It may consist of only a few lines hastily drawn. You will not have to hide it in your desk, taped to the back of a drawer. That is pointless. But don't leave it out to be seen, thinking no one will know what it is. It will be taken for scribble and thrown in the wastebasket or be carefully folded and idly shredded by a friend one night during a conversation. You might want to write only a set of numbers down in one corner of a piece of paper and underline them. **When you try to find a place for it**—a place not too obvious, not too well hidden so as to arouse suspicion—**you will begin to understand the futility of drawing maps.** It is best in this case to get along without one, although you will find your map, once drawn, as difficult to discard as an unfinished poem.)

First go north to Tate. Go in the fall. Wait in the bus station for an old man with short white hair wearing a blue shirt and khaki trousers to come in on a Trailways bus from Lanner. You cannot miss him. He will be the only one on the bus.

Take him aside and ask him if he came in from Molnar. Let there be a serious tone to your words, as if you sensed disaster down the road in Molnar. He will regard you without saying a word for a long time. Then he will laugh a little and tell you that he boarded the bus at Galen, two towns above Molnar.

His name is Leon. Take him to coffee. Tell him you are a journalist, working for a small paper in North Dakota, that you are looking for a famous desert that lies somewhere west of Tate, **a place where nothing has ever happened.**

Tell him you wish to see the place for yourself.

If he believes you he will smile and nod and sketch a map for you on a white paper napkin. Be careful. The napkin will tear under the pressure of his blunt pencil and the lines he draws may end up meaning nothing at all. It is his words you should pay attention to. He will seem very sure of himself and you will feel a great trust go between you.

You may never again hear a map so well spoken.

There will be a clarity in his description such that it will seem he is laying slivers of clear glass on black velvet in the afternoon sun. Still, you will have difficulty remembering, especially the specific length of various shadows cast at different times of the day. Listen as you have never listened before. It will be the very best he can do under the circumstances.

Perhaps you are a step ahead of me. Then I should tell you this: a tape recorder will be of no use. He will suspect it and not talk, tell you he must make connections with another bus and leave. Or he will give you directions that will bring you to your death. Make notes if you wish. Then take the napkin and thank him and go.

You will need three or four days to follow it out. The last part will be on foot. Prepare for this.

Prepare for the impact of nothing.

Get on a regimen of tea and biscuits and dried fruit. **On the third or fourth day, when you are ready to quit, you will know you are on your way.** When your throat is so thick with dust that you cannot breathe you will be almost halfway there. When the soles of your feet go numb with the burning and you cannot walk you will know that you have made no wrong turns. When you can no longer laugh at all it is only a little further. Push on.

It will not be as easy as it sounds. When you have walked miles to the head of a box canyon and find yourself with no climbing rope, no pitons, no one to belay you, you are going to have to improvise. When the dust chews a hole in your canteen and sucks it dry without a sound you will have to sit down and study the land for a place to dig for water. When you wake in the morning and find that a rattlesnake has curled up on your chest to take advantage of your warmth you will have to move quickly or wait out the sun's heat.

You will always know this: others have made it. The man who gave you the map has been here. He now lives in a pleasant town of only ten thousand. There are no large buildings and the streets are lined with maples and a flush of bright flowers in the spring. There is a good hardware store. There are a number of vegetable gardens—pole beans and crisp celery, carrots, strawberries, watercress and parsley and sweet corn—growing in backyards. The weather is mixed and excellent. Leon has many friends and he lives well and enjoys himself. He rides Trailways buses late at night, when he is assured of a seat. **He can make a very good map with only a napkin and a broken pencil.**

He knows how to avoid what is unnecessary.

ONLY SMALL STONES ROLL ALONG IN THE WATER;

THE BIG ONES LET THE WATER GO BY.

— SPOKEN BY A NAVAJO INDIAN IN A DREAM

12   Black Mesa with the Sagrada Familia Church, San Ildefonso Pueblo, New Mexico

BETWEEN NOSTALGIA AND SUSPICION:

THE NEW PLACES OF ART

I am indebted to Paul Rainbird, a Native American leader and activist from the San Ildefonso Pueblo in New Mexico, for the insights he gave me into the Tewa religion as we strolled along the dusty pathways of his pueblo's main square, which is not far from the Catholic church built by the Spanish at the time of their conquest. Rainbird described a cosmic analogy whereby the serpent, an earth force, unites with lightning, energy from the heavens: "We feel we are the keepers of the energy and our ceremonies are done for the benefit of the whole universe," he explained. At the time, I was reminded of the mystical concept of *axis mundi* and of the ceremonial pueblo dancer who symbolically connects the earth and the sky in order to reflect the unity of things. The valiant struggle of the Native American peoples to preserve their ancestral knowledge is intimately linked to nature and resounds even in their proper names: For example, in a beautiful metaphor Lightning Basket (Tsigowanu Tun), Rainbird's sister's name, combines the starkness of atmospheric phenomena with the receptiveness of a container crafted by human hands.

At one of Cochiti Pueblo's ritual festivities, traditional costumes and cuisine coexist with drinks, T-shirts, and sneakers that display logos from widely known commercial brands. During the ceremony, dancers' feet mark a rhythm akin to the systole and diastole of a gigantic heart, seemingly amplifying the movements of growing corn or the pattern of rain. I watched this magical rite and sensed that there was some strange truth in that conjunction among the forces of the universe. Not far from the pueblos, scientists at the Santa Fe

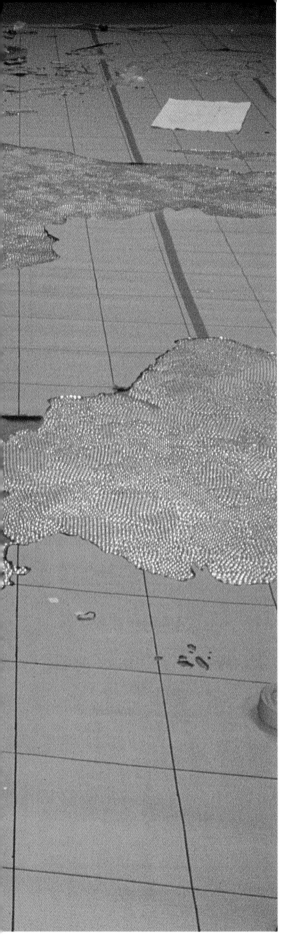

Institute investigate theories of chaos and resort to the most advanced technologies to find orderly, meaningful patterns that underlie unpredictable natural phenomena. Science, like religion or poetry, strives to identify relationships that shed light on the meaning of matter in the universe. Like art, or any other human construction, these disciplines are linked to various power structures.

Today, many forms of power and exploitation are changing the world's cultural and economical landscapes. In Santa Fe, New Mexico, for example, the romanticization of the desert along with vestiges of Hispanic colonization and subsequent Anglo-Saxon domination have conspired to produce an exotic theme park fueled with contradictions. New roads have been built around Santa Fe to carry atomic waste to one of America's largest dump sites, while luxurious mansions in the vast landscape have become repositories for exquisite collections of old and contemporary art. This paradoxical ensemble reveals one of the elemental premises of the American Dream—that of the West as a land of conquest, needing to be made lucrative as well as productive. Mythical American cartography continues to have the West running along a vanishing line where fantasies of travel, conquest, and freedom converge, and where every man can find his own intimate desert. In one of her writings, the nuclear physicist Vandana Shiva recalls that President Theodore Roosevelt explained that the colonizer and the settler had justice on their side because it was not possible to keep "that great continent as merely a hunting preserve for scruffy savages."[1] From another angle, the philosopher Milton J. Tornamira, paraphrasing Gilles Deleuze, who in turn quoted Leslie Fiedler, wrote that the unconscious of the American Dream has been imprisoned by two traumas: the Native-American genocide and African-American slavery.[2]

Nowadays, when racism, xenophobia, and other politics of exclusion and exploitation are still very much present; when the media turns even pain into spectacle; and when self-styled democratic governments sacrifice their own citizens to dangerous scientific experiments, the role of the artist cannot simply be reduced to creating beautiful objects viewed in immaculate museum rooms. The impenetrability of the institutions that uphold artistic canons and compartmentalize knowledge is

Mona Hatoum, *Map*, 1998, during installation

reluctantly giving way to new hybridizations that open gateways to unexplored territories. The authority and limitations of Modernism, as well as the once-glorified autonomy of art, have been challenged from within by theories of suspicion and from without by the growing anxiety of those who have lived on its fringes. Feminist misgivings, post-Colonial thought, or the deconstruction of art's own aesthetic dogmas have driven art along new roads where the integration of form, content, and social function is more thorough.

Some of the fundamental charges of the contemporary artist are to arouse critical awareness and to enlighten us with new visions. The artist may be a healer, an inventor of worlds, a worker who activates social relationships, a researcher seeking lost paradises, an electrician generating new connections, a theoretician studying cultural identities and their displacements, or a laborer dismantling the hermetic constructions of the powers that be. Art must become the driving force behind thought, a generator of pleasure, and the catalyst for new political practices. In this context, a curator could be conceived as an editor seeking the best syntax for linking artworks, but also as an agitator promoting exhibition as a place of confrontation and exchange between the artist and the community. These roles serve to explore specific problems and to combat the desire to regiment and uniformly consume the same cultural fetishes.

An exhibition is a conjunction of energies, an articulation of ideas that are in constant negotiation between the institution, the curator, and the artist. Once installed, the exhibition is received by the public and the media, who interpret and connect it to other areas of knowledge through their own preconceived ideas, experiences, and sets of values. Today's biennials provide new contemporary models for exhibitions and are widely used for stimulating intercultural dialogue, promoting quality tourism, and placing cities on the competitive map of international prestige. They are also billed as a fluid alternatives to the inviolable solidity of museums. Fully aware of these determinants, I decided to invite, for SITE Santa Fe's third biennial, a number of artists from diverse cultural contexts. These artists questioned the current development of art and took into account the specificity of the place where this exhibition was to be held, with all its concomitant uncertainties and contradictions.

Multiculturalism has served as a temporary device for appeasing guilt over Colonial domination and has helped to reveal other ways of producing beauty not prescribed by Western paradigms. While today globalization promoted by transnational capitalism seeks out others' exoticism so that every distinguishing gesture can be stereotyped, a dual aesthetic of mirrors is giving way to a multi-focal aesthetics of prisms. The 29 artists participating in *Looking for a Place* are courageous surveyors of these issues. They have given their utmost using

First Atomic Bomb Explosion, July 16, 1945, White Sands, New Mexico

available means and are well aware, once this adventure is over, that they will pursue new analyses, new forms of cultural exchange and coexistence, and a continued respect for differences. In the search for new standards of imparting knowledge and distributing power and wealth, art can become a privileged form of resistance, action, and hope.

Rosa Martínez
Curator
Looking for a Place
SITE Santa Fe's Third International Biennial

1 Maria Mies and Vandana Shiva. *Ecofeminismo: Teoría, crítica y perspectivas.* Barcelona: Icaria, 1997.
2 Milton J. Tornamira. *Tientos sobre el tema del caos y la experimentación vital.* Santiago de Compostela: Universidad de Santiago de Compostela, 1993.

Rosa Martínez (center) with Carl Michael von Hausswolff (left) and preparator Jaime Hamilton (right) in door frame, surrounded by members of La Sala de la Sociedad de San José (from left to right): Joe Anaya, Manuel Anaya, Elias Sena, Robert Anaya, and Michael Anaya

ENTRE LA NOSTALGIA Y LA SOSPECHA:

LOS NUEVOS LUGARES DEL ARTE

He de agradecer a Paul Rainbird, un dirigente y activista indio de la reserva de San Ildefonso Pueblo, en Nuevo México, que me acercara a las visiones de la religión Tewa mientras paseábamos por la polvorienta esplanada de la plaza de su pueblo, en la que descansa la kiwa ceremonial no lejos de la iglesia católica que construyeron los españoles durante la época de su dominación. Rainbird describió la analogía cósmica que une a la serpiente, como fuerza de la tierra, con el relámpago, como energía del cielo. "Sentimos que somos los guardianes de la energía y nuestras ceremonias se celebran en beneficio del mundo entero," dijo Rainbird. Recordé el concepto de *axis mundi* y al danzante ceremonial del Pueblo que contecta simbólicamente la tierra y el cielo para rememorar la unidad de todas las cosas. La denodada lucha de los pueblos indios por preservar su saber ancestral guarda una intensa relación con la naturaleza y resuena en sus propios nombres. El de la hermana de Rainbird, Tsigowanu Tun—Cesto de relámpagos—condensa en una bella metáfora la terribilidad de los fenómenos atmosféricos y la receptividad de las construcciones humanas.

En una de las fiestas rituales del Cochiti Pueblo, los trajes y la comida tradicional convivían con las bebidas, las camisetas y las zapatillas deportivas de las marcas comerciales más publicitadas. Durante la ceremonia, los pies de los danzantes marcaban el ritmo como la sístole y la diástole de un corazón gigantesco y parecían amplificar los inaudibles movimientos del crecimiento del maíz o reproducir los sonidos de la lluvia. Contemplé ese rito de magia simpatética y sentí que había una extraña verdad en esa conjuración de las fuerzas del universo. No lejos de los pueblos, los científicos del Santa Fe Institute investigan las teorías del caos y, con las más avanzadas tecnologías, buscan patrones que den sentido y orden a los imprevisibles fenómenos de la naturaleza. La ciencia, como la religión o la poesía, quiere descubrir relaciones que iluminen el sentido de la materia del universo y que incrementen nuestro propio poder para propiciar sus fuerzas. Como el arte u otras producciones humanas, la ciencia, la religión y el lenguaje están ligados a diferentes estructuras de poder.

Hoy, otras formas de explotación están cambiando los paisajes económicos y culturales del mundo. En Santa Fe de Nuevo México, por ejemplo, la romantización

del desierto, las huellas de la colonización hispánica y la posterior dominación anglosajona han configurado un exótico parque temático y un centro turístico de primera magnitud. En los alrededores de Santa Fe se han construido nuevas carreteras para enterrar los desechos atómicos en uno de los basureros más importantes de Estados Unidos mientras selectas mansiones perdidas en el paisaje guardan bellísimas colecciones de arte antiguo y contemporáneo. En este paradójico conjunto anida uno de los polos fundamentales del Sueño Americano: el del Oeste como tierra de conquista que el capital ha de hacer lucrativa y productiva. En la cartografía mítica Americana, el Oeste sigue siendo una línea de fuga donde conviven las fantasías del viaje, la conquista, la aluci-nación y la locura, y donde cada uno puede encontrar su "desierto íntimo." La física nuclear Vandana Shiva cita en uno de sus escritos como el presidente de Estados Unidos Theodore Roosvelt decía que el colonizador y el pionero habían tenido la justicia de su lado porque no era posible mantener ese gran continente como una mera reserva de caza para salvajes desharrapados.[1] Desde otra pers-pectiva, el filósofo Milton J. Tornamira, parafraseando a Gilles Deleuze, que citó a Leslie Fiedler, afirma que el inconsciente del Sueño Americano está aún aprisionado entre dos traumas: el del genocidio indio y el de la esclavitud de los negros.[2]

Hoy, cuando el racismo, la xenofobia y otras políticas de exclusión y explotación aún siguen activas; cuando los medios de comunicación de masas convierten incluso el dolor en espectáculo; cuando gobiernos autodenominados "democráticos" inmolan a sus propios ciudadanos en peligrosos experimentos científicos, la labor del artista no puede reducirse únicamente a crear bellos objetos que se contemplen en las inmaculadas salas de los museos. El hermetismo de las instituciones que definen el canon artístico y compartimentan los saberes va dejando lugar —no sin resistencias— a nuevas hibridaciones que abren las puertas hacia territorios inexplorados. La autoridad y los límites de la Modernidad, así como la otrora glorificada autonomía del arte, se han visto desafiadas: desde dentro por las teorías de la sospecha y desde fuera por la creciente ansiedad de los que han vivido en sus márgenes. Los cuestionamientos feministas, el pensamiento poscolonial o la deconstrucción de sus propios dogmas estéticos hacen que el arte derive por nuevos caminos en los que se integran más equilibradamente forma, contenido y función social.

Una de las responsabilidades primordiales del artista contemporáneo es despertar nuestra conciencia crítica e iluminarnos con nuevas visiones. El artista puede ser un curandero, un inventor de mundos, un trabajador que activa las relaciones sociales, un investigador que busca paraísos perdidos, un electricista que genera nuevas conexiones, un teórico de las tensiones entre las identidades y los desplazamientos culturales, un obrero que desmantela las construcciones herméticas de los poderes dominantes. El arte ha de ser motor del pensamiento, generador de placer e inductor de nuevas prácticas políticas. El curador es entonces un editor que busca la mejor sintaxis para interconectar las obras, pero es también un agitador que promueve la exposición como un lugar de confrontación e intercambio entre el artista y la comunidad, tanto para explorar problemas específicos como para combatir la uniformación del deseo por consumir los mismos fetiches culturales.

Una exposición es una conjunción de energías, una articulación de ideas que han de ser constantemente negociadas entre la institución, el curador y el artista. Una vez configurada, el público y los medios la reciben interpretándola como un texto que leen conectándolo con otras áreas de su saber, con sus ideas preconcebidas, sus propias experiencias y sus sistemas de valores. Hoy las bienales son un modelo de exposición ampliamente utilizado para estimular los diálogos interculturales, para promover un turismo de calidad y para situar a las ciudades en el competitivo mapa del prestigio internacional. Se plantean también como una alternativa fluída a la solidez sacramental de los museos. Plenamente consciente de esta lógica, al preparar *Looking for a Place*, la Tercera Bienal Internacional SITE Santa Fe, decidí invitar a una serie de artistas que, proviniendo de diversos contextos culturales, se estuvieran cuestionando los actuales devenires del arte a la vez que tenían en cuenta la especificidad del lugar donde la exposición se celebraba, con todas las contradicciones e incertidumbres acumuladas en él.

El multiculturalismo ha servido temporalmente como pantalla para paliar un relativo sentimiento de culpa por la dominación colonial, pero ha ayudado también a descubrir que hay otras formas de producir belleza no determinadas por los paradigmas occidentales. Aunque la globalización promovida por el capitalismo transnacional busca que "los otros" hablen sólo de su exotismo para convertir en estereotipo cualquier gesto de las diferencias, hoy la estética dual de los espejos está dejando paso a la estética multifocal de los prismas. Los 29 artistas participantes en *Looking for a Place* han sido oteadores arriesgados de estas problemáticas, han dado lo mejor de sí mismos con los medios existentes y saben que tras esta aventura seguirán construyendo nuevos análisis, nuevas formas de intercambio cultural, de convivencia y de respeto de las diferencias. En la búsqueda de nuevos modelos para la producción del saber y la distribución del poder y de la riqueza, el arte puede ser una forma privilegiada de resistencia, de acción y de esperanza.

Rosa Martínez
Curadora
Looking for a Place
Tercera Bienal Internacional SITE Santa Fe

1 Maria Mies and Vandana Shiva. *Ecofeminismo: Teoría, crítica y perspectivas.* Barcelona: Icaria, 1997.
2 Milton J. Tornamira. *Tientos sobre el tema del caos y la experimentación vital.* Santiago de Compostela: Universidad de Santiago de Compostela, 1993.

Yolanda Gutiérrez, *The river whispers to us,
and the snake hisses*, 1999, during installation

Lake at San Ildefonso Pueblo

TO THE HEROES

PUBLIC, PRIVATE, AND SACRED PLACES

Since our first biennial in 1995, each of SITE Santa Fe's three international biennials has been a unique project arising from the conceptual vision of a curator who, in concert with artists from around the world, responds not only to our institution and the Southwest region, but also to global issues. Following the themes of the first two biennials—identity and the individual in 1995's *Longing and Belonging: From the Faraway Nearby* and identity within society in 1997's *Truce: Echoes of Art in an Age of Endless Conclusions*—Rosa Martínez and the artists selected for SITE Santa Fe's 1999 Third International Biennial, *Looking for a Place*, addressed issues of place and its meaning in contemporary life. Ideas related to globalization, the speed of communication, rapidly changing political and social priorities, and the ways in which "universes" exist in even the smallest areas of the world, were explored by 29 artists who represent 23 countries.

When we appointed Rosa Martínez to curate SITE Santa Fe's third biennial, one of the most exciting aspects of her proposal was that she and several of the artists wanted to extend the exhibition beyond the parameters of the museum's building into public and sacred spaces in and around the Santa Fe area. Given that expanding into the community was one of the original premises for the SITE Santa Fe biennials, and that Martínez was highly successful in using multiple venues, including public and historic sites, when she curated the Istanbul Biennial in 1997, we were invigorated by the challenges of integrating this exhibition into nontraditional places.

Martínez conceived *Looking for a Place* as an exhibition that would examine international issues in the context of Santa Fe, which provided a backdrop that includes the legacy of Native American and Spanish Colonial culture and history as well as Los Alamos's Manhattan Project. This diverse heritage, which is still a primary cultural force in and around Santa Fe, informed and shaped many of the projects in the exhibition. Martínez, who is based in

Charlene Teters, *Obelisk: To the Heroes*, 1999, during installation

New Mexico State Capitol building

Barcelona, Spain, brought a rich perspective to this curatorial project through her Spanish heritage, unique vision, and experiences at other international exhibitions.

One of the most significant aspects of this biennial exhibition was the extent to which it engaged and involved the community. While the heart of the biennial was located in the 18,000-square-foot SITE Santa Fe space, the off-site venues and collaborators—La Sala de la Sociedad de San José de Galisteo, the San Ildefonso Pueblo and its council, the Los Alamos Airport, Santa Fe Community Television, the Santa Fe Budget Inn, the New Mexico State Capitol building, the Sandoval Municipal Parking Garage, the City of Santa Fe and the Trust for Public Land, the Santa Fe Southern Railway Station, and Our Lady of Guadalupe parish and its historic cemetery—permitted art to merge into the places where residents live and work, and where tourists venture.

By situating art in nontraditional places, viewers were given the opportunity to interact in different ways with the art, and to experience it by virtue of the associations a particular place evoked. Whether private, as in the "white cube" space of the museum; public, as in the landscape, the parks, the old dancehall in Galisteo, or the Los Alamos Airport; sacred, as in the cemetery of the Our Lady of Guadalupe church or the San Ildefonso Pueblo; or somewhere in between, the spaces influenced not only the creation of the art, but also the interpretation of it. What emerged from this biennial was an acute awareness of how place can affect the viewer's perception of an artwork.

Looking for a Place challenged the traditional spaces of museums or galleries, which, although they are technically public spaces, essentially feel private. They are places where art is isolated, distinct from the viewer, and where a certain degree of reserve is typically expected. However, the gap between the art and the viewer is bridged to some extent when a viewer is asked to participate to "complete" the artwork. For example, within the SITE Santa Fe building, installations of work by Lygia Clark and Francisco Ruiz de Infante, among others, disrupted expectations of the viewers who, via participation, became more than onlookers. As viewers tried on masks and goggles or squirmed through a rubber tunnel in Clark's installation; or, in Ruiz de Infante's installations, climbed ladders and squeezed into storage spaces, where they watched the artist's videos and spied on audiences in the main galleries of SITE Santa Fe's building, they became active participants who created their own specific and highly individual experiences of the artwork. That is not to say artwork requires physical participation in order for it to provide an unconventional experience, but this kind of interaction certainly has become one of the ways to shock the established though often static relationship between art and viewer.

As the exhibition moved outside the museum to diverse off-site locations in and around Santa Fe proper, engagement with the community became more complex and met with both positive and negative response. Organizing many of these off-site projects proved a stimulating but often difficult process, and our efforts to negotiate terms, attain permissions, and assist artists in the execution of their projects were greeted with varying results. Few proposals were met with any kind of enthusiasm, and in several cases funds had to change hands before projects could begin. Benevolent support of the projects was surprisingly rare in our community, perhaps because of a general distrust of art in the public arena and the corresponding potential controversy.

In order for public art to have power, it must be placed in a situation or location that allows viewers to come upon it randomly, almost by chance, but within the context of their everyday lives. One highly successful example of this kind of project and placement is Charlene Teters's *Obelisk: To the Heroes*, which was sited in front of the New Mexico State Capitol building. Her monumental sculpture—an obelisk formed from adobe and embedded with mementos from people living in the Santa Fe community—is the counterpoint to the historic monument in Santa Fe's Plaza that was dedicated, in 1868, to honor the "...heroes who have fallen in the various battles with savage Indians in the territory of New Mexico." Teters's *Obelisk*, which clearly exploits the irony of the original monument's dedication in an area in which Native Americans compose a significant portion of the population, records a history that is more inclusive of all peoples. This obelisk is completely at home in front of the capitol building, and as of October 2000, nearly a year after the biennial's close, it still stands in place and has become an important stop for tourists when they visit Santa Fe.

Ghada Amer's biennial project, *Love Park*, which was located in the vacant lot adjacent to SITE Santa Fe's building, featured park benches that were cut in half and repositioned so the halves faced in opposite directions. Flanking these benches were the traditional green parks department signs made untraditional by their messages. Instead of "Do Not Litter" or "Park Closes at Dusk" these signs featured phrases about love, gender, and relationships from varied texts. Amer's *Love Park* became an interactive site for art—a site in which the viewer, who might under normal circumstances relax in a park setting, instead was provoked by the positioning of the benches and the messages on the signs.

Other off-site projects were located where the line between public and private places is blurred. Diller + Scofidio's *Room 120*, a multimedia installation, was located in a motel room at the Santa Fe Budget Inn, a block from SITE Santa Fe. Rather than changing the motel room to suit their piece, the artists capitalized on the associations it would evoke. Specific areas—such as the closet, the space beneath the bed, and a bedside table drawer containing a bible—were disturbed by mechanical devices, thus drawing attention to the "motel-ness" of the room. Surveillance cameras observed these areas and generated images that continually screened on the room's television.

The Diller + Scofidio piece raises interesting questions and possibilities about spaces. Motel rooms are spaces that are both public, in that they are accessible to anyone who pays the price of "admission," and private, in the sense that for the duration of a visit, the generic room becomes home to its occupant—a place in which the most personal of activities are performed. Is a motel room in fact more private than the museum spaces we typically regard as private? Might, in some cases, a motel room be considered a sacred space—a place in which people have the freedom to honor that to which they are committed?

Art situated in places that are public but also sacred to many—such as religious sites, church cemeteries, and pueblo land—caused controversy and raised the question of whether it is sacrilegious or disrespectful to introduce contemporary art on such sites. Proper permission had been obtained from the Our Lady of Guadalupe parish for Carl Michael von Hausswolff's project *Red Light*, which bathed the church's cemetery in red light after sundown. And while initial response to the piece was positive, one passerby complained that the project was disrespectful and sacrilegious. Although previous agreements had been reached, the church's parishioners responded to the complaints by requiring that the piece be shut down.

In another incident, despite the permissions that had been received after elaborate negotiations with the San Ildefonso Pueblo council and tribal member Paul Rainbird, who acted as an intermediary, pueblo elders complained about Yolanda Gutiérrez's installation on the pueblo's lake. *The river whispers to us, and the snake hisses*, which took the shape of a snake and was constructed with blue and yellow corn, was meant to symbolize the spiritual kinship between Native American and Mesoamerican cultures. The piece was literally ripped out of the lake during the opening weekend of the biennial when elders objected to its presentation on sacred Native land.

In both of these cases, art sparked objections from people who were more concerned with the sacred quality of the space than the work of art itself. In many ways Teters's piece can be seen as more subversive than either von Hausswolff's or Gutiérrez's installations. However, that its placement—and that of Ghada Amer's *Love Park*, von Hausswolff's *Dancehall Séance* at the old Galisteo dancehall, Simone Aaberg Kærn's Los Alamos Airport project, or several other off-site projects—was on a public rather than sacred site left it less open to objection on the basis of religious or political beliefs.

Once art is situated *beyond* a designated museum space and objections are raised, it becomes more difficult to use the defense often given about controversial work, such as that by Robert Mapplethorpe or Andres Serrano, that is displayed *within* museums: "If you don't like it, don't look at it." Of course, the demand to pull down two works of art is an act of censorship, but this is just one of the difficulties that will have to be confronted as art becomes ever more political and as it moves into spaces that are not only public but also sacred. Inviting artists to create site-specific artwork in places where it might not be expected creates both the difficulty and the excitement of new possibilities. When context and place enhance the meaning of an artwork, as they evidently did for several biennial pieces, it is highly rewarding for artists, curators, and audiences alike.

I would like to thank all of the participating artists and Rosa Martínez for their commitment to *Looking for a Place*. I am especially privileged to have the complete confidence and support of board president Bobbie Foshay-Miller and the entire SITE Santa Fe Board of Directors. Many thanks to Frieda and Jim Arth, whose generosity and tireless efforts during the opening events were invaluable. I extend my heartfelt appreciation to SITE Santa Fe's entire staff and group of interns, volunteers, docents, and exhibition preparators, who were pulled in so many directions in the course of organizing and presenting this major exhibition: Their skills, talents, and dedication are irreplaceable. I also thank our major supporters including The Brown Foundation, Inc., Houston, The Burnett Foundation, The Dunlevy-Milbank Foundation, Inc., Lannan Foundation, LLWW Foundation, McCune Charitable Foundation, The Rockefeller Foundation, Sotheby's and Sotheby's International Realty, Agnes Gund and Daniel Shapiro, and Jim Kelly of James Kelly Contemporary, who organized the SITE Unseen Benefit Auction.

SITE Santa Fe dedicates this catalogue to the memory of Jodi Carson, one of our first employees, whose commitment to our museum remains truly inspirational. I extend my thanks to Sandy and Dr. Richard Carson for their continuing support of our institution through the Jodi Carson Memorial Fund.

Louis Grachos
Director
SITE Santa Fe

ARTISTS' PROJECTS

HELENA **ALMEIDA**

GHADA **AMER**

JANINE **ANTONI**

MONICA **BONVICINI**

LOUISE **BOURGEOIS**

TANIA **BRUGUERA**

CAI GUO-QIANG

LYGIA **CLARK**

DILLER + SCOFIDIO

DR. GALENTIN **GATEV**

GREENPEACE

YOLANDA **GUTIÉRREZ**

MONA **HATOUM**

CARL MICHAEL VON **HAUSSWOLFF**

CARSTEN **HÖLLER**

SIMONE AABERG **KÆRN**

ZWELETHU **MTHETHWA**

NIKOS **NAVRIDIS**

SHIRIN **NESHAT**

RIVANE **NEUENSCHWANDER**

GABRIEL **OROZCO**

PIPILOTTI **RIST**

FRANCISCO **RUIZ DE INFANTE**

BÜLENT **ŞANGAR**

ARSEN **SAVADOV** / GEORGY **SENCHENKO**

CHARLENE **TETERS**

SERGIO **VEGA**

MIWA **YANAGI**

Note: Numbers accompanying captions indicate the position of art within SITE Santa Fe's building and its exterior surroundings. See the parcours map on page 112 following the artists' projects.

Cai Guo-Qiang, *Calling*, 1999, during installation

33

I have never come to terms with canvas, paper, or any other support. I believe that what has made me come forward out of these elements through using volumes, shapes, and string is my deep dissatisfaction with problems of space. Either by facing these problems or refuting them, they have become the one constant of my work. I believe that I can say now that I paint paintings and that I draw drawings. It is not a question of exhibiting but rather exposing, and also of being able to communicate more deeply the ideology and character of "art"—accepting it and therefore being able to deny it.

Through photographs within drawings I believe that the same denial is made in a variety of ways. What I am exposing is not the "artist's imprints," but rather the representation and the denial of these imprints.

This denial means a rediscovery of another space while it also tumbles into another poetic trap. This happens because by placing myself as the "artist" in a real space and the spectator in a virtual space he exchanges places with the support and becomes imaginary space.

To become an unreality. To become an appeal to the possession of intimate joys. To become at rest as in the drawings. To live the warm interior of a curved line. To meet again the peace of an inhabited drawing.

— **Helena Almeida**

[This text was first published in conjunction with a solo show of the artist's work in 1976 at the Sociedade Nacional de Belas-Artes, Lisbon, Portugal.]

(26)
above and opposite page inset: *Inhabited Drawing*, 1977

opposite: *Inside of Me*, 1998

HELENA **ALMEIDA**

GHADA **AMER**

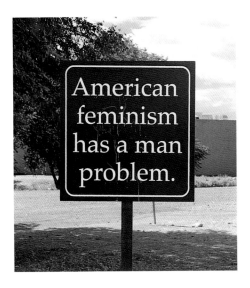

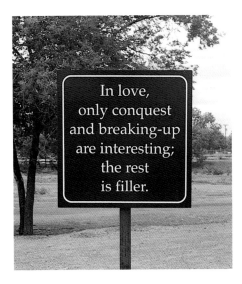

Love Park was an outdoor piece. It was situated in the plot next to SITE Santa Fe surrounded by a McDonald's, a railroad, a gas station, and a mountain in the faraway. I very much liked this space because it is a meeting point for the homeless, for solitary people walking their dogs, and because it carries the sad feeling elicited from something broken. I wanted to add something usually found in a park, such as benches.

I reconnected 10 benches that had been cut in half so that the halves faced in opposite directions. Unlike a loveseat they were set back-to-back. I organized and cleaned the spaces where the cut benches were placed,

configured a promenade, and installed each set between two trees like a Romantic tableau from the 19th century. While looking out to the landscape and sitting on the cut benches, we could read quotations about love and life taken from books I read and liked. These quotations appeared like the indications we find in public parks that mention the rules of behavior one should follow. Each pair of quotations was meant to suggest a dialogue between two people who are talking to each other without listening, and the sequence, as a whole, was a walk through the incomprehensibility of love.

— **Ghada Amer**

JANINE **ANTONI**

and is a sculpture consisting of two 800-pound limestone boulders that were placed on top of one another, with a steel pole acting as a central axle. A second pole was then inserted into the top rock, parallel to the ground—similar to a mill. I pushed the pole around in a circle five hours a day, for six weeks. With great effort, I worked to achieve a relationship in which the two forms resisted and gave into one another at an equal rate. I stopped grinding when the rocks became interconnected.

— Janine Antoni

(24)
and, 1997–99, installation view and detail

39

(10)
*What does your wife/girlfriend think
of your rough and dry hands?*, 1999,
installation view and details

MONICA **BONVICINI**

Optional: Date of birth.............. Place of birth................. Occupation..............

1 Do you see your work as being creative?

yes

2 Do you remember all the buildings you have worked on and do you view them differently than other buildings?

yes – everyone of them
Yes – I view the ones I worked on differently

3 Why do you think construction workers are almost always men?

Hard, physical, dangerous, dirty work.
What you wear to work isn't as important as the work you do.

4 Is construction work masculine?

Yes, most construction workers are men.
See Webster's Dictionary.

5 Why did you choose this work?

wanted to work outside and be part of a team

6 Could you tell a typical construction worker joke?

What is a typical construction worker joke?
Construction workers aren't typical.

7 What does your wife/girlfriend think of your rough and dry hands?

I have soft hands.

8 What is so appealing about construction workers?

Appealing to whom?
I don't find anything appealing about construction workers.

9 How do you get along with your gay colleagues? *I don't have any gay colleagues.*
I would probably get along fine if they worked hard and kept their political agenda at home.

10 Do you think there is anything erotic about building materials or in the process of construction?

no

11 Would you consider designing a building yourself?

yes

12 Which word is most used on construction sites?

"Building" (Build, built)

13 Whom would you like to wall up? *Nobody, they would tear up the wall getting out and I would have to rebuild the wall.*
– Maybe these High School kids that are nuts and wanting to kill people.

What does your wife/girlfriend think of your rough and dry hands? focuses on the parameters of gender and architecture.

I conceived questionnaires that aimed at people on the front lines of the construction process. These forms were distributed at construction sites in Germany, Italy, and the US, with the help of architects and contractors. The distribution itself mirrored a chain of command inherent to the power structure of the trade. The results, enhanced with photographs of construction sites I took over the last eight years in different countries, were presented in book form along with the original questionnaires in three languages.

Though at first glance the ironic tone of the questions seemed merely a joke to some workers, the consolidated results of the questionnaires do, in fact, truly reflect the real environment of gender and work.

I thought it would be interesting to take a look at architecture and gender through someone else's eyes, rather than through those of theorists, architects, or consumers. I was looking for an intimate and humorous study of the people who build the walls you cook, live, and fuck in.

— Monica Bonvicini and Jan Ralske

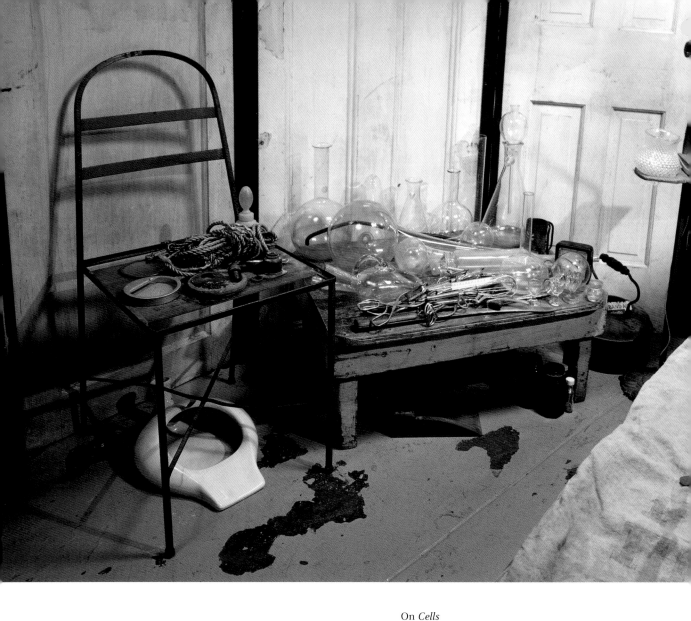

On *Cells*

The subject of pain is the business I am in.
To give meaning and shape to frustration and
suffering. What happens to my body has to be
given a formal abstract shape. So you might
say, pain is the ransom of formalism.

The existence of pains cannot be denied. I
propose no remedies or excuses. I simply want
to look at them and talk about them. I can't
make them disappear; they're here to stay.

The *Cells* represent different types of pain:
the physical, the emotional, and the psychological, and the mental and intellectual. When
does the emotional become physical? When
does the physical become emotional? It's a
circle going around and around. Pain can begin
at any point and turn in either direction.

Each *Cell* deals with fear. Fear is pain.
Often it is not perceived as pain, because it
is always disguising itself.

(22, 23)
Cell I, 1991, installation details

LOUISE **BOURGEOIS**

Each *Cell* deals with the pleasure of the voyeur, the thrill of looking and being looked at. The *Cells* either attract or repulse each other. There is this urge to integrate, merge, or disintegrate.

In bed, crouching in fear, the person in one of these *Cells* is hiding. What he is hiding is his state of sickness. He is physically sick and afraid of death. But it is not that simple; he has other fears. What is not justified is his fear of people knowing about his sickness. He is afraid of not having any friends or afraid of losing those he has.

Some diseases are considered shameful because others associate them with sin. So he is intensely possessive of his privacy and fears the onlookers. He fears people are trying to pry into his privacy. Yet he is projecting his fear of being seen, for he himself is a voyeur, a latent voyeur. This is expressed with the windows.

If you can look out, they can look in. The clear glass represents no secrets.

Sick people die of the need of companionship, a stroking hand, a hungering for compassion. He runs away from people, and people run away from him out of fear of contagion. So he is isolated by his own fear and by that of others.

The transparent glass represents a sickness. When you're sick, people don't like you; you're not desirable. My mother was ill and used to cough up blood; I helped her to hide her illness from my father.

— **Louise Bourgeois**

[First published in 1991 by the Carnegie Museum of Art, Pittsburgh, Pennsylvania, in the exhibition catalogue for the *Carnegie International, 1991/1992*.]

My work is a response to my cultural environment—a fusion of the personal and intimate with the collective and social in order to reflect upon culture, politics, ideology, and identity. In this way, the work is focused on the relationship between art and power, on change and human transformation as part of that dynamic.

The materials I use include dirt and mud, spit, rocks, meat, lambs and lambskin, coffee, cotton, marble, letters and photographs, textiles, human hair, paper, wood, and objects lost and found on the streets of Havana.

Ritual, myth, obsessive repetition for cathartic purposes, the fallacy of utopian proposals, intuition, death, and contemplation are all part of the structure of the series, *The Burden of Guilt*. Most recently, I have been focusing on submission and obedience as acts of social survival.

— Tania Bruguera

(17)
The Burden of Guilt, 1999, performance views

TANIA **BRUGUERA**

A lighthouse was erected on the roof of SITE Santa Fe's building. It used materials like household and industrial trash, as well as discards from nature, such as fallen tree branches. The shape and structure of the tower incorporated architectural elements from the local Native American culture.

The objects placed on the exterior of this lighthouse are those used by the people who habitually reside inside these types of functional structures. Its light blinked off and on, as if calling to a faraway time when the desert plateau was once part of the ocean. This displaced lighthouse on top of the museum seemed a bit funny, yet, at the same time, when one saw its light going on and off, one sensed the isolation of today's civilization, particularly in relation to contemporary art.

— Cai Guo-Qiang

(1, 14)
Calling, 1999, installation views and detail

CAI GUO-QIANG

LYGIA **CLARK**

We Are the Proposers

We are the proposers: We are the mould, it is up to you to breathe the meaning of our existence into it.

We are the proposers: Our proposition is that of dialogue. Alone we do not exist. We are at your mercy.

We are the proposers: We have buried the work of art as such and we call upon you so that our thought may survive through your action.

We are the proposers: We do not propose you with either the past or the future, but the now.

— Lygia Clark

[Originally published in *Livro-obra*, 1983, a collection of the artist's writings.]

(25)
top: *Goggles*, 1968
center: *Breathe With Me*, 1966
bottom: *Water and Shells*, 1966

opposite: *The I and the You*, 1967

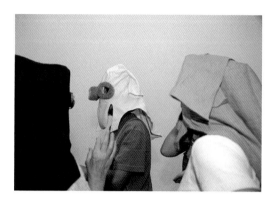

LYGIA **CLARK**

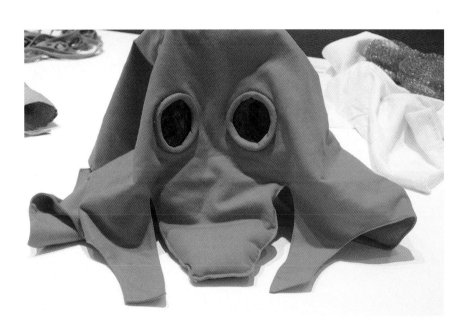

top: *Pumpkin-Colored Sensorial Mask,* 1967
below and opposite: installation views with
participants, 1999

UFO sitings, Marlboro ads, road movies, serial killing sprees, nuclear testing grounds, classified military sites, the Western film genre—the facts and fictions of the American Southwest have long fed the collective imagination. The vast scale of its unpopulated landscape engenders a "paranoid sublime." Conversely, the phenomenon of the chain motel brings the comfort of familiarity to every site no matter how geographically remote or culturally diverse.

The intersection between a generic, featureless room in a Santa Fe motel and the mythic desert that surrounds it was the point of origin for the installation. *Room 120* at the Santa Fe Budget Inn was wired with closed-circuit microsurveillance cameras. The live cameras recorded a variety of banal sites in the room at close range: the closet, the bible shelf, the compressed space beneath the bed, etc. Each of these sites was subtly disturbed through a mechanical device. The scaleless images perpetually sequencing through the room's TV monitor produced a sublime of the hyperbanal.

— **Diller + Scofidio**

DILLER + SCOFIDIO

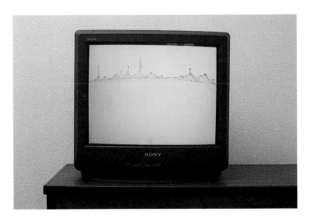

Room 120, 1999, installation view and details

Santa Fe Budget Inn

DR. GALENTIN **GATEV**

Over several months, I observed the transportation difficulties faced by four rural priests from the region of Botevgrad in Bulgaria, 60 kilometers from the capital city Sofia. I watched their motor vehicles and followed their movements through the area, which I then selectively documented on videotape.

I chose a parking garage in downtown Santa Fe as the site for this piece. Two adjacent parking spaces were encased in a sheetrock structure with a rolling garage door. Over the entrance, a frieze-like installation with individual images of each priest suggested panels from an altarpiece. In the left parking space, four documentary videotapes ran simultaneously on a screen divided into quadrants; at right, on a round tabletop, a priest puppet on a motorcycle continuously circled on a special set of elliptical tracks.

— **Dr. Galentin Gatev**

Motor Engines with a Regional Purpose, Evidence, 1998, installation view and details

Sandoval Municipal Parking Garage

(2, 3)
above: *End nuclear threats*, placement of
5,000 crosses at Bohunice Nuclear Power Plant,
Czech Republic, to commemorate the fifth
anniversary of the accident at Chernobyl Power
Plant, Ukraine, 1991

opposite: *Blood on the ice from seal cull*,
Newfoundland, Canada, 1981

Greenpeace started as a small group of individuals
intent on standing up to the corporate and industrial
giants that dominate the world. Its worldwide members are motivated by the will to defend the earth as
a place that we all share and that must be preserved
beyond state divisions. Greenpeace activists contribute
to the deconstruction of the myth that modern science
and technology are the great liberators of mankind—
a myth that has defended terrible technological and
humanitarian crimes under the rhetoric of progress.
Greenpeace does not limit itself to mere words in its
struggle to defend certain collective ideals. Many of
its eloquent actions comprise an aesthetic perspective and could be considered performances or installations. In this manner, it implements Joseph Beuys's
concept of "social sculpture" meant to alter people's
awareness. The actions of Greenpeace erase the fron-
tiers that separate art and life. The decision to invite
Greenpeace to participate in SITE Santa Fe's biennial
is representative of the ways in which the essence of
art and its social role are expanding.

— **Rosa Martínez**

GREENPEACE

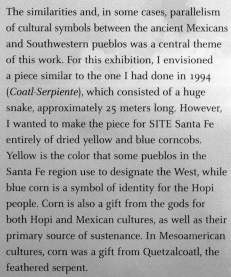

The similarities and, in some cases, parallelism of cultural symbols between the ancient Mexicans and Southwestern pueblos was a central theme of this work. For this exhibition, I envisioned a piece similar to the one I had done in 1994 (*Coatl-Serpiente*), which consisted of a huge snake, approximately 25 meters long. However, I wanted to make the piece for SITE Santa Fe entirely of dried yellow and blue corncobs. Yellow is the color that some pueblos in the Santa Fe region use to designate the West, while blue corn is a symbol of identity for the Hopi people. Corn is also a gift from the gods for both Hopi and Mexican cultures, as well as their primary source of sustenance. In Mesoamerican cultures, corn was a gift from Quetzalcoatl, the feathered serpent.

I fastened the corncobs, in groups of 24, to strips of metallic mesh that were made to float

The river whispers to us, and the snake hisses, 1999, installation view

Lake at San Ildefonso Pueblo

YOLANDA **GUTIÉRREZ**

with plastic tubes. I then attached these modules to form an articulated model that, with the flow of wind, drifted in an undulating manner across the surface of the water. This piece originated from my desire to construct a work of monumental dimensions that could be placed in a lake or river, or more specifically a body of water belonging to a pueblo near Santa Fe. The San Ildefonso Pueblo was the most accessible site due to its proximity to Santa Fe as well as its hospitality toward tourists.

I conceptualized this work as a new symbol of kinship between Native North American and Mesoamerican cultures—cultures that remain linked despite physical separation. Though our cultures have been threatened with extinction since the Spanish conquests by territorial divisions, technological progression, and perhaps recently by cultural globalization, we are still of the same origins and of the same thread. We have common philosophies, upbringings, and traditions—a reason for being and a mission within the cycle of life that must not be forgotten.

In this piece I wanted to both rescue and record certain symbols through memory, and to propagate and honor these symbols—simple images of wildlife that are beautiful in and of themselves—that have been handed down to us through the teachings of our past as well as the traditions of other cultures.

For the Native North Americans as well as the pre-Hispanic Mexicans, nature is a holy manifestation of the soul in its totality, an indescribable spirit. As such, we understand its depth and approach it with respect. We can learn by observing the intricate laws and images of nature, and through the most simple and poetic of events—the whispering of water, the flight of the eagle, or the zigzagging of the snake.

— **Yolanda Gutiérrez**

[The tribal council had initially agreed to allow Yolanda Gutiérrez to install her work at the lake on the San Ildefonso Pueblo. However, during the opening weekend of the biennial, several of the elders at the pueblo objected to its presence, and the piece was removed immediately.]

59

MONA **HATOUM**

Map developed out of a series of floor works I began making in 1995 based on the rug, mat, or carpet as a form. In these works I sought to destabilize the surface of the ground by rendering it simultaneously seductive and treacherous. With *Map*, I expanded this idea of "shaky ground" to include the entire earth. The piece consists of a large expanse of transparent marbles spread across the floor in the shape of a map of the world. The surface of the map is entirely level, as if an earthquake had equalized every landmass. The political borders are intentionally ignored, and only the continents are delineated. Yet, they exist in a state of disintegration as the marbles roll around and get knocked out of place whenever people walk across the space. The surface of this map is physically unstable and threatening to the people around it, but those same people also constantly threaten the piece's existence. Whereas in the past we may have imagined the world as stable, solid ground, we now acknowledge the delicate fabric of life in an uncertain and shifting world.

— **Mona Hatoum**

(6)
Map, 1998, installation view

following spread: installation detail

MONA **HATOUM**

CARL MICHAEL VON **HAUSSWOLFF**

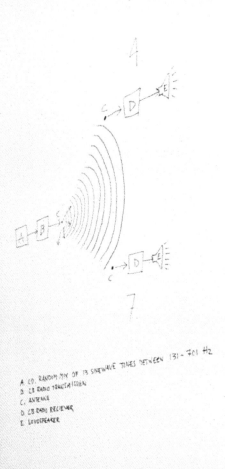

The tones have a social and practical use. Frequencies at large are mostly unexplored. How do they work? What effect do they have on life? The debate on whether cell phone frequencies can cause cancer and other maladies continues, and we still don't even know what frequencies were used in collapsing the town of Jericho, what frequency the Chinese considered the "base" tone for life in general, or if the daily noise volume in cities has lessened our perception or our auditory abilities to listen to contemporary music. The installation *Operation of Spirit Communication (New Mexico Basic Minimalism Séance)* enables people/souls to communicate with the living, but it does not want to prove that souls are able to communicate through these 13 sinewaves via radio frequencies. Rather, it wants to underscore alternative forms of function and usage. It points out that everything is possible and that nothing is absolute.

(21, Plan B Evolving Arts)
Operation of Spirit Communication (New Mexico Basic Minimalism Séance), 1999, installation view

Galisteo Dancehall Séance, 1999, installation view

La Sala de la Sociedad de San José de Galisteo

CARL MICHAEL VON **HAUSSWOLFF**

The configuration of the old dancehall in
Galisteo, which had not been used in 30 years,
functioned perfectly for *Galisteo Dancehall
Séance.* The entrance lies at one end of the
building, and the stage at the other. On either
side, the interior walls are lined with a singular
unbroken bench. A mix of old American and
Mexican dance music coupled with the hum of
the dancehall's electricity (60 hertz) was heard
through a pair of speakers hung from the ceiling,
as well as visualized via an oscilloscope in
wave-like patterns from a video projection on
the stage's back wall. The detection of earlier
and other life forms was evident.

Red Night, 1999, installation view
Our Lady of Guadalupe Cemetery

CARL MICHAEL VON **HAUSSWOLFF**

In *Red Night*, the cemetery of Our Lady of
Guadalupe church was flooded with 22,000
watts of deep red light—a monochrome surface activating various functions of memory.

— Carl Michael von Hausswolff

[Though approval of the site for *Red Night*
had been obtained from the church's priest
and its parish council, as well as the Don Diego
Neighborhood Association, the piece was
dismantled shortly after its installation due
to the objections of a Santa Fe resident.]

69

A sketchy retrospective of Carsten Höller's previous creations shows that the tendency to always be moving toward a goal or some other state of being is not only the theme of *New World*, but is something that threads its way throughout all of his artistic thoughts. The goal of this pursuit is called the *New World*, happiness, or *Skop*, and can also simply be called the future. The nature of this goal remains conspicuously vague, whereas the striving forward that has been described is incandescent, manifold, and ambivalent.

In Carsten Höller's narrative there are many not-to-be overlooked insinuations that human feelings, the will, psychological characteristics, or whatever can be called "the subject," is not necessarily a product of the spiritual or mental, but is linked to processes in the human brain that can be scientifically explained by neurological research—even if the "difficult problem" of how to really explain how we experience phenomenon cannot be solved. It is a view of things that, without assigning them any value, effects a demythologization of feelings and visions, allowing them to be seen as naturalized appearances. Scientific insights about the body and the spiritual/mental state that have been made in the fields of molecular genetics, evolution theory, and neurological research are the basis for such a shift of perception. For some time these insights have crossed over the borders of expertise and have gradually attained social and cultural meaning. Their consequences for ethics and anthropology have become a topic of wider discussion.

— Theodora Vischer

[Selected excerpts from the essay "New World," included in the catalogue for Carsten Höller's *New World* exhibition, 1998–99, Moderna Museet, Stockholm, Sweden, and Museum für Gegenwartskunst, Basel, Switzerland.]

(16)
above: *Sphere*, 1998, installation view

opposite: *Crows and Lederhosen*, 1999, installation view

CARSTEN **HÖLLER**

SIMONE AABERG KAERN

While our mental ability to fly is almost unrestricted, actual physical flying requires technological support and includes the risk of confronting the unexpected. Simone Aaberg Kærn's artistic research—which involves intriguing mixtures of fantasy and reality, theory and practice—has driven her to become an aviatrix.

In her video *Royal Greenland*, Kærn explores both the desire to fly and the physical requirements that make flight possible. Through a combination of technology and gymnastics, she simulates unassisted flying. On the monitor, images of her body appear as they traverse natural and urban landscapes in unexpected trajectories.

For her project at the Los Alamos Airport, *Camping in the clouds*, Kærn invited visitors on an actual flight in a Piper Cub airplane. She has also discovered the stories of many unrecognized World War II women pilots and has memorialized them in a compelling series of portraits.

Kærn illustrates the quirky relationships between art and life, the mystical and the technological, as well as the irony of machinery that both allows for the viewing of outstanding natural beauty and suggests modern warfare. Most significantly, she has shown how trust and freedom acquired through these radical flying adventures can lead to new ways of experiencing pleasure that originate in the intensity and pulse of life.

— **Rosita Valiente**

(7)
Royal Greenland, 1995, video stills

Camping in the clouds, 1999,
performance views and video stills

Los Alamos Airport

SIMONE AABERG **KÆRN**

Camping in the clouds…miles away from SITE.

The assignment was clear from the beginning. Rosa Martínez hired me to find a way and a place to make unassisted human flight possible. I chose Los Alamos, which is situated in a beautiful location high on a mountain—a site almost reaching into the heavens. It was the perfect location, a secret peak inhabited by scientists. I wanted all the available brains there to work for me like they did for Oppenheimer when the ultimate cloud was created, as a side effect to the nuclear blast.

— Simone Aaberg Kærn

ZWELETHU **MTHETHWA**

These photographs focus primarily on the psychological shift that we experience when a space is converted and rearranged, and thus has a new function and a new meaning attached to it.

I depict these shifts by photographing rooms that have been converted into church-like environments. Due to lack of space and economic constraints, people in South Africa, especially from the rural areas, have been forced into building homes as informal structures by employing recycled materials such as posters, newspapers, corrugated iron, and mud. On Sundays, the very same homes are transformed into churches.

These interiors manifest poignant tensions in the dualities of purpose and function that are illustrated, for example, in a cupboard that serves as altar, in a kitchen or dining room as church—in the individual home as a collective place of worship. The resulting images become windows into a complex cultural transit.

— **Zwelethu Mthethwa**

(8)
Some Sacred Homes, 1999

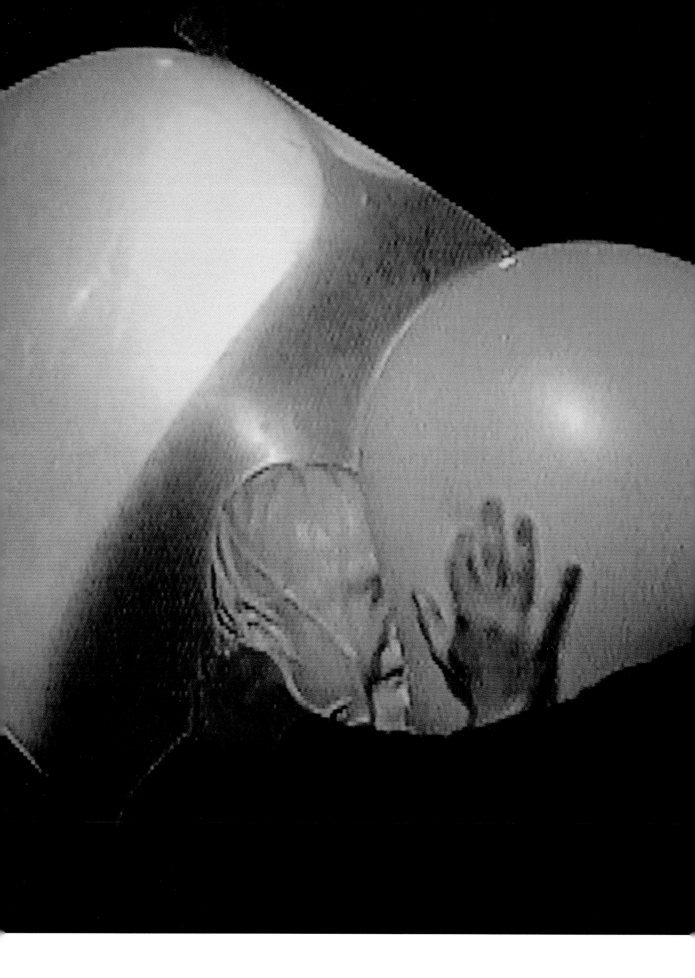

NIKOS **NAVRIDIS**

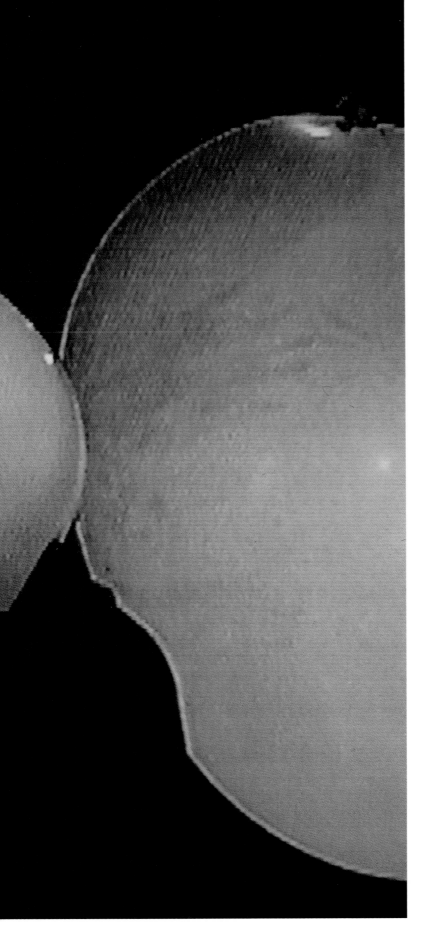

The people in my videos are blind. They move around the environments, wearing replicas of themselves, in the form of latex heads made from molds of their own heads. When they are inside the replicas, they can see nothing. They have acquired blindness. Blindness is a requirement; it is one of the "materials" I use in this work. The other materials are touch, predetermined movements, breath, and latex.

The people in my videos do not imitate situations; as they are not actors, they do not know how to do such a thing. They are located within a situation whose characteristics they do not know. Quite literally, they are faced with a situation.

For me, the words "space" and "place" are very close in meaning. And just as there cannot be space without movement, the place that I was seeking was an evolving space. It was a constantly shifting boundary. As a result, the "space" and the "boundary" were often the same.

Ultimately, what the word "place" made me look for was the commonplace: a point with an infinite number of multiplicities and an infinite number of possible solutions.

The original idea was to move from A to B and back. What I was looking for was not simply a shift in position. I wanted a completed movement, a revolution. Each completion presupposes a return. This was something dictated by the work itself: a return each time we are looking for a place, whenever and in whatever way we do so.

— **Nikos Navridis**

(20)
Looking for a Place from *The Question of the Age of the Void* series, 1999, video still

(15)
Rapture, 1999, video still

SHIRIN **NESHAT**

Rapture, 1999, video stills

The situation of women under Islam is, one might say, the occasion of *Rapture*. But *Rapture* rises to a universal level of humanistic allegory, making it significant for us all. It is, moreover, a good example of what one would look for in identifying contemporary masterpieces. Its currency is assured by the technology of the video projection, which did not exist when the canon of great art was formed. But there is something almost timeless in the action. The narrative itself could have been enacted in the remote past.

SHIRIN NESHAT

"From the beginning," Neshat says, "I made a decision that this work was not going to be about me or my opinions on the subject, and that my position was going to be no position. I then put myself in a place of only asking questions but never answering them."

— Arthur C. Danto

[Excerpt from "Pas de Deux, en Masse," an article on Shirin Neshat in *The Nation*, June 28, 1999.]

(19)
Common Place, 1999, installation view
and installation process

RIVANE **NEUENSCHWANDER**

The project consisted of an installation made with talcum powder swept on the floor.

Two rectangles were outlined on the floor with adhesive tape, which was removed at the end of the process. Some talcum powder was spread within these empty rectangles and then swept with an ordinary broom. A thin layer of powder was subsequently formed on the floor by the act of sweeping. After the adhesive tape was removed, the rectangle remained clearly defined by this "coating" of white powder. The excess talcum powder was gathered into small piles that were placed just off-center, inside the rectangles. The traces of the broom remained present and testified to the act of sweeping.

The installation was transformed with the passing of time as it incorporated the process of disappearance through the accumulation of daily dust, which slowly covered and blended with the layer of talcum powder on the floor, becoming one in the end.

— Rivane Neuenschwander

I like to see my work as the result or a byprod-
uct or a leftover of specific situations. That's
probably why I cannot separate photography
from my sculptural practice. I don't know in
advance whether I will need to use photography
or whether the work will, in the end, become
an object. What I am doing, how it ends up
as a sign, is all about language, but sometimes
it becomes a physical thing; sometimes it is
just photography.

I always think of my photography like a
shoebox, and in that sense I really think it's
irrelevant if it's a huge photomural or if it's a
small place. You can travel through space and
time, be transported; the size doesn't matter.
I don't see any sculptural attributes to photography. These attributes are in relation to what
is happening and if the idea is strong enough
in terms of time and space.

(18)
From Dog Shit to Irma Vep, 1997, video stills

GABRIEL **OROZCO**

In everyday reality, you have objects that you can look at but that you cannot touch. You can touch a table, a pen . . . all these levels of reality are just accepted. In my own work, I was connecting all these levels, hand and body—relationships with these objects and the ideas behind language, action, sign, and collapsing them all together. I was making decisions in terms of how to display these objects, how to activate a space in the art world, in galleries and museums, apart from the street, my house, and my everyday life. So I started to activate the work using these different levels. It's true that I move with some flexibility through different practices of sculpture, and that I consider myself a sculptor. Drawings and photographs are also activating the space in different ways, but I always think that they are related to the sculpture.

"Space" happens when the sign is moving in life, or when the language is in action and when the spectator, the activator of the sign, enacts these relations in which knowledge, passion, sign, language, perception, and sexuality intervene. That is when space starts to be perceived in a more comprehensive, more total way. When you are in front of something that just covers all your attention, you generate that space and you are experiencing the world in a total way; that's perhaps the space that contemporary sculpture, and maybe art in general, tries to generate.

— **Gabriel Orozco**

[Selected excerpts from an interview with Benjamin Buchloh originally published in the catalogue for the exhibition *Clinton is Innocent*, 1998, Musée d'art moderne de la ville de Paris.]

Looking for a Place (TV Program), 1999, video stills

Santa Fe Community Television, Channel 6

PIPILOTTI **RIST**

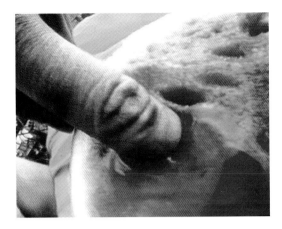

The TV tube is the flame thrower
The room is the maelstrom
And you are the pearl inside
We're flying through the wired suburbs. The world in front of
and behind the TV set is the biggest video installation around.
We shoot our neighbors, and so we recapture space and house
from the TV screen. The more openly and viciously we eye each
other, the more brilliant the pictures. Nothing can affect us now
unless they cut off the power.

— Pipilotti Rist

(11)
Mixing the Air (Sabotage), Zone 2: Curiosity,
1999, installation view

FRANCISCO **RUIZ DE INFANTE**

For the past several years, all the works that I have produced—films and installations—are organized around a sequence of events or physical environments that the spectator has to experience in order to discover—by way of a strange game of clues—the intellectual ideas presented.

This means of constructing a work originated from my attempts to manufacture situations that summon childhood fears and simultaneously evoke the danger and subconscious magic that these situations generate. However, in an increasingly clear manner, my pieces meditate on forms of "interactive freedom" that contemporary society offers us. Each new work is constructed to suggest an ironic or grave likeness to our "point-and-click" society—an apparently loosely controlled society—that calls to mind an "interactive game" with very precise rules.

In most of my installations the spectator is an integral part of the work—a participant rather than an external element that contemplates or analyzes it. The presence of this actor/viewer is indispensable. His or her attitudes and body movements, whether anticipated or not, complete the work.

In *Mixing the Air (Sabotage)*, I was hoping that moving through typically inaccessible spaces and opening doors or climbing up precarious staircases would create moments of confusion for the actor/viewer.

As its title suggests, this project reflects on the idea of danger or the need for sabotage—the fear and fascination with the knowledge of, and control over, certain "vital systems." The insurance waiver, for instance, which required the participants' signatures before they could enter the installation, created a control that simultaneously imbued the participant with an expectation or intuition of risk. The compulsory act of this signature reveals the extent to which our modern Western societies—and American society in particular—obligate us to demonstrate, by means of an official document, that we are responsible for our own acts—that is, that we are responsible adults. This lack of personal "responsibility" and "trust" implied by the law demands a hyperprotective system that sometimes reaches the level of the absurd.

— **Francisco Ruiz de Infante**

Mixing the Air (Sabotage), Zone 1: Place for Secret Activities, 1999, installation view

FRANCISCO **RUIZ DE INFANTE**

top: *Mixing the Air (Sabotage), Zone 3: Control,*
1999, installation view
bottom: *Mixing the Air (Sabotage), Zone 4:*
Learning, 1999, installation view

93

The landscapes I choose are places where the fabric and roads of the city intersect with rural migration and inherent applications of religious practice and rituals.

The radical urban transformation and speed of new life depicted in these settings is arrested in my photographic compositions. I integrate individual images into larger sequential works so that the urban geography is turned into a consistent and coherent space.

In these works a moment of questioning, of doubt, is frozen. It is the moment at which the traditions and faith of the believer are set in opposition to the requirements imposed by urban and contemporary life. It leaves one to contemplate various scales of violence and sacrifice, from the most restrained to the bloodiest.

— **Bülent Şangar**

(9)
Feast of Sacrifice, 1997–99

BÜLENT ŞANGAR

ARSEN **SAVADOV** / GEORGY **SENCHENKO**

The artistic debut of Arsen Savadov and Georgy Senchenko occurred at the end of the 1980s. With the Soviet era not yet over, they joined an international fashion trend that focused on a return to painting. Savadov and Senchenko's huge canvases from this period feature strange and hallucinatory subjects painted in aggressive colors that are referential, irrational, hypervisual, and erotic.

In the Ukraine, critics referred to Savadov and Senchenko's works as neo-Baroque (the 17th-century Baroque is, in fact, associated with the Ukrainian artistic tradition). Even when Savadov and Senchenko moved away from painting toward interactive performance, video, and other art forms typical of the 1990s, they continued to be influenced by the neo-Baroque imagination. In 1994 they

realized a grandiose and provocative curatorial project titled *Landscape of Cultural Revolution*. The works of various young artists were fenced off from the public and made visible only through reversed binoculars attached to holes in the fence. This approach is characteristic of Savadov and Senchenko's body of work: On the one hand it explores the phenomenon of vision and its possibilities; on the other, it reacts to the much-debated "crisis of representation."

In 1996, as a part of *Manifesta 1* at the Bojmans van Bojmingen Museum in Rotterdam, Savadov and Senchenko exhibited their "toilets project" for the first time. Short phrases such as "To the smiles of the sweet ones" and "To peace in the whole world" appeared in the museum's bathrooms above

(13)
Arsen Savadov, *Donbass-Chocolate*, 1997

urinals and sinks. Though this strategy was symptomatic of the critique of institutions and utilized a minimal aesthetic, it preserved the artists' devotion to Baroque's high rhetoric.

In their most recent work, Savadov and Senchenko have returned to representative art through the photographic medium. As in the earlier pieces, they display visual lavishness, erotic provocation, and a sophisticated referentiality. *Donbass-Chocolate*, however, is a project of social research, a response to the collapse of a symbolic order prevalent in post-Communist societies—not an apologia for artistic autonomy. In these photographic images, diverse emblematic codes collide: nouveau-riche glamour with Ukrainian national mythology, neodecadent eroticism with fragments of the grand style of Stalinist culture.

—Viktor Misiano

(27)
Welcome, 1996–99, installation details

ARSEN **SAVADOV** / GEORGY **SENCHENKO**

for breaking ties — big and small

for confirmation in their solitude

(28)
Untitled, 1998

Within many American Indian creation stories, the place of our coming forward, our creation, is referred to as Turtle Island. Indigenous people have a close connection to the earth, especially our homelands. To open up the earth—for any reason, even to plant seeds—is a powerful act. American Indian artisans who use clay for their art forms conduct songs and prayers before gathering up clay for pottery vessels or sculptures. The owning of earth—the act of claiming land and drawing borders around a piece of earth—was a foreign concept to my ancestors.

Both the obelisk and the flag raising at Iwo Jima celebrate and are also, in their moment of execution, acts of claiming land from others. "To the heroes who have fallen in various battles with savage Indians in the territory of New Mexico" is inscribed on one of the panels from The Soldiers' Monument in the Santa Fe's main plaza. *Obelisk: To the Heroes* was conceived as a reaction to this monument and installed in front of the New Mexico State Capitol building. It is constructed with adobe bricks that have been imbedded with personal mementos donated by members of the public. Each person who participated in bringing and implanting the objects, keepsakes, toys, and other personal objects is part of the history of the piece. In a fundamental way, these object-laden bricks are metaphors for a community's history, artifacts, presence, and human rights.

Mound: To the Heroes is partially filled with earthen forms made as references to human bodies, mass graves, or to generations of bodies going back to the earth. At one end of the earth mound is the focal point of the installation: a photomural of the flag raising at Iwo Jima. In this version all the flag raisers have been removed except a Pima man named Ira Hayes, who later died on his reservation in Arizona from exposure to the elements. The juxtaposition of this Native American with the American flag becomes a metaphor for indigenous peoples' continued struggle for basic human rights in this country.

The ironies of heroism and defeat and celebration and remorse resonate between the two installations—humanizing, demystifying, and connecting past, present, and future.

— **Charlene Teters**

(4)
Mound: To the Heroes, 1999, installation view

CHARLENE TETERS

CHARLENE **TETERS**

Obelisk: To the Heroes, 1999, installation view
and details

New Mexico State Capitol building

Picnic: The Golden Age with Mosquitoes, 1999,
installation view and detail

Back in the hotel, the rays of afternoon sun
were sliding over the shining pots and tropical
plants of the front patio, illuminating and
shading the peach wall as in a Baroque compo-
sition. I sat down on the hammock hanging
in the patio and tried to imagine the interior
of the church I had failed to enter earlier.

As I began to fall asleep I found myself
before Caravaggio's Christ. He was heavy,
like a sacrificed animal, and his dirty feet
announced that he had been walking in the
market among the odors, the flies, and the
yelling. Immersed in a world of shadows, I
felt the weight of his body in my arms. Then
I heard laughter: It was Velázquez's drunks.
Their shining red noses glittered while they
made their toasts, staring straight at the camera.
I realized that these vine-leaf-crowned drunks

SERGIO **VEGA**

had completely taken over everyday space, and that Bacchus, who once could only be found in those places reserved for the sacred, now visited them as just another friend from the bar. It was boiling hot as I entered the bucolic forest of a Flemish landscape. A group of bashful, robust women aired their fragile skin among the fruits and the buzzing of harvest flies. Observing the scene was Rubens's red parrot. Eve grabbed the forbidden fruit. Tiepolo's sky enraptured me with an instantaneous outburst of luminous, changing clouds. The New World was born as plumed Indian women entered mounted on enormous crocodiles, and then I was overwhelmed by dizziness as I was shot from a giant cornucopia and found myself rolling among the fruits laid out on Carmen Miranda's headdress. I was lost in a world of representations that had sprung to life and overtaken the real world with a strange mixture of fantastic geography and supernatural history.

Falling asleep in the hammock, in my last waking moment I envisioned a golden age with mosquitoes. It was a form desired by everyone, an ultimate moment that never came true but that expanded in new possibilities, each time getting closer to Paradise. It was a virtual return to the Paradisum Voluptatis, the site of voluptuous forms, where the body is one with the whole.

The European Baroque, even with all its vulgar naturalism, fell short in a number of ways. It lacked the concrete texture of perspiration—that intimate battle with humidity—the monumentality of spaces, the exuberance of vegetation with the smell of ripe fruits, the exotic flowers in the never-ending heat, those sunburned colors, and the buzzing mosquitoes, which, like fat angels from a tropical rococo, rule without mercy in the sky of Eden.

— Sergio Vega

[Excerpt from "Day 4" of the artist's diary, *El Paraíso en El Vuevo Mundo*.]

SERGIO **VEGA**

Picnic: The Golden Age with Mosquitoes, 1999, details

(5, 29)
Elevator Girl House 1F, 1997

The vanishing point in my work describes an obsession with moving further ahead.

My preliminary landscapes evolve from aimless walks through buildings and empty commercial spaces; my personal landscapes are composed from the memories of these meanderings.

I am also interested in the ambiguous "passages" that lie between interior and exterior—such as the street arcade, which is neither inside nor outside, public nor private—as well as transient consumer spaces with specific perspectives, places that existed before department stores or malls were created.

MIWA **YANAGI**

My work depicts an arrested state—a frozen utopia—in which department stores and arcades appear continuous. These images, however, underscore the absence of fluidity and the impermanence of space inherent to city life, like street culture that always comes and goes.

The characters who appear in my work are merely symbolic; they exist without will or individuality. But those defects, in a way, are mesmerizing. There is a fashion of imitation among the figures that causes them to gradually blend into each other, as in a beehive, where there is no singular identity.

Department stores and shopping malls were strategically designed to instigate consumption. Though these environments may seem visually engaging and energetic, they can be suddenly transformed into decadent spaces. Products are multiplied and indiscriminately copied through limitless marketing. This subdivision of variation is similar to the multiplication of a flower. But if you are satiated by all of these products, then the world simply becomes monotonous.

I walk around the city, at first pulled into the dreams offered by these consumer spaces, and then suddenly awakened from them. At that moment, the scenery I have been looking for appears.

— **Miwa Yanagi**

Eternal City 1, 1998, installation views

Santa Fe Southern Railway Station

opposite: Interstate 25 between Santa Fe
and Albuquerque

MIWA **YANAGI**

MAPPING of the EXHIBITION

SITE SANTA FE BUILDING AND EXTERIOR SURROUNDINGS

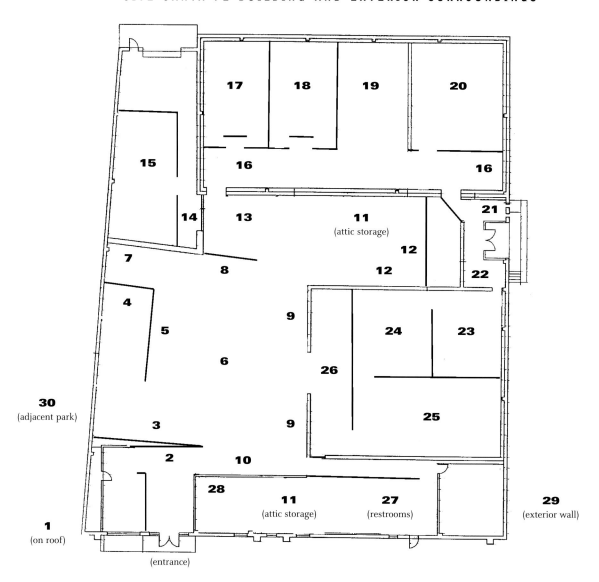

(1, 14) **CAI** GUO-QIANG

(2, 3) **GREENPEACE**

(4) CHARLENE **TETERS**

(5, 29) MIWA **YANAGI**

(6) MONA **HATOUM**

(7) SIMONE AABERG **KÆRN**

(8) ZWELETHU **MTHETHWA**

(9) BÜLENT **ŞANGAR**

(10) MONICA **BONVICINI**

(11) FRANCISCO **RUIZ DE INFANTE**

(12) SERGIO **VEGA**

(13) ARSEN **SAVADOV**

(15) SHIRIN **NESHAT**

(16) CARSTEN **HÖLLER**

(17) TANIA **BRUGUERA**

(18) GABRIEL **OROZCO**

(19) RIVANE **NEUENSCHWANDER**

(20) NIKOS **NAVRIDIS**

(21) CARL MICHAEL VON **HAUSSWOLFF**

(22, 23) LOUISE **BOURGEOIS**

(24) JANINE **ANTONI**

(25) LYGIA **CLARK**

(26) HELENA **ALMEIDA**

(27, 28) ARSEN **SAVADOV** / GEORGY **SENCHENKO**

(30) GHADA **AMER**

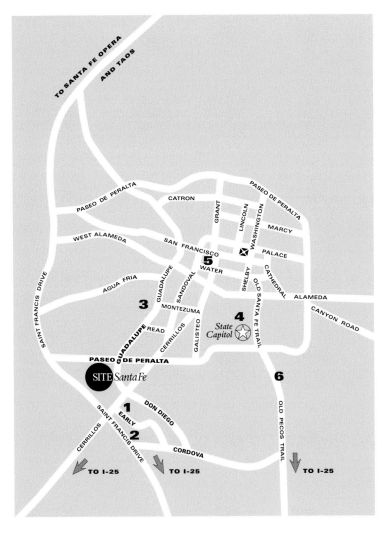

OFF-SITE VENUES

(1) **Santa Fe Budget Inn**
DILLER + SCOFIDIO

(2) **Our Lady of Guadalupe Cemetery**
CARL MICHAEL VON HAUSSWOLFF

(3) **Santa Fe Southern Railway Station**
MIWA YANAGI

(4) **New Mexico State Capitol building**
CHARLENE TETERS

(5) **Sandoval Municipal Parking Garage**
DR. GALENTIN GATEV

(6) **Plan B Evolving Arts**
CARL MICHAEL VON HAUSSWOLFF

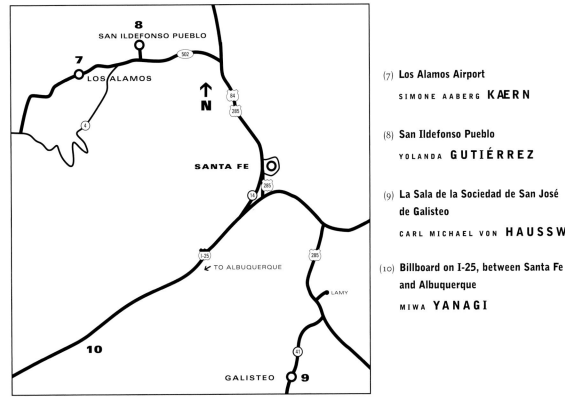

(7) **Los Alamos Airport**
SIMONE AABERG KÆRN

(8) **San Ildefonso Pueblo**
YOLANDA GUTIÉRREZ

(9) **La Sala de la Sociedad de San José
de Galisteo**
CARL MICHAEL VON HAUSSWOLFF

(10) **Billboard on I-25, between Santa Fe
and Albuquerque**
MIWA YANAGI

CHECKLIST

HELENA ALMEIDA

Inhabited Drawing, 1977
(Desenho habitado)
6 photographs, horsehair
16 x 20 inches each
Courtesy of the artist and the Luso-American
    Development Foundation Collection, Lisbon, Portugal

Inside of Me, 1998
(Dentro de mim)
14 photographs
23 x 34 inches each
Collection of the artist

Inside of Me, 1998
(Dentro de mim)
photograph
73 x 48 inches
Collection of the artist

GHADA AMER

Love Park, 1999
20 signs, 10 cut benches
variable dimensions
Site-specific project produced by SITE Santa Fe
Courtesy of the artist and Deitch Projects,
    New York, New York

JANINE ANTONI

and, 1997–99
2 800-lb. limestone boulders, steel rod
approximately 5 x 3 x 3 feet
Courtesy of the artist and Luhring Augustine,
    New York, New York

MONICA BONVICINI

*What does your wife/girlfriend think of
your rough and dry hands?,* 1999
books, questionnaires
Funded by SITE Santa Fe; the Italian Cultural
    Institute of Los Angeles, California; Galleria
    Emi Fontana, Milan, Italy; and the artist
Courtesy of the artist; Mehdi Chouakri Gallery, Berlin,
    Germany; and Galleria Emi Fontana, Milan, Italy

LOUISE BOURGEOIS

Cell I, 1991
mixed-media installation with found objects,
    clothes, furniture
7 x 8 x 9 feet
Courtesy of the artist and Cheim & Reid,
    New York, New York

Untitled (Two Chairs), 1998
steel and glass sculpture
11 x 12 x 8 inches
Courtesy of the artist and Cheim & Reid,
    New York, New York

TANIA BRUGUERA

The Burden of Guilt, 1997–99
(El peso de la culpa)
performance, 5-minute video projection
Courtesy of the artist

CAI GUO-QIANG

Calling, 1999
lighthouse composed of industrial and
    natural refuse
approximately 20 feet high
Site-specific project produced by SITE Santa Fe
Courtesy of the artist

Calling, 1999
7 ink drawings of artist's initial
  biennial proposal
13 x 19 inches each
Courtesy of the artist

LYGIA CLARK

(Following works are of variable dimensions)

Breathe With Me, 1966
(Respire comigo)
rubber tube

Draw With Your Finger, 1966
(Desenhe com o dedo)
plastic, water

Hand Dialogue, 1966
(Diálogo de mãos)
elastic Möbius strip

Ping-Pong, 1966
(Ping-Pong)
plastic, ping-pong balls

Sensorial Book, 1966
(Livro sensorial)
plastic, shells, pebbles, elastic

Stone and Air, 1966
(Pedra e ar)
plastic, stone, elastic

Water and Shells, 1966
(Água e conchas)
plastic, water, shells

Cesarean, 1967
(Cesariana)
plastic, paper

The I and the You, 1967
(O eu e o tu)
fabric, plastic, water, rubber

Sensorial Masks series, 1967:
(Máscaras Sensoriais)

> *Black Sensorial Mask*
> *(Máscara sensorial preta)*
> fabric, polystyrene, metal, mirror,
>   fragrance

> *Blue Sensorial Mask*
> *(Máscara sensorial azul)*
> fabric, plastic, polystyrene, shell,
>   fragrance

> *Cherry-Colored Sensorial Mask*
> *(Máscara sensorial cereja)*
> fabric, polystyrene, metal, fragrance

> *Green Sensorial Mask*
> *(Máscara sensorial verde)*
> fabric, shell, sand, fragrance

> *Pumpkin-Colored Sensorial Mask*
> *(Máscara sensorial abobora)*
> fabric, plastic, sand, gourd, fragrance

> *White Sensorial Mask*
> *(Máscaras sensorial branca)*
> fabric, steel wool, polystyrene, fragrance

Abysmal Masks, 1968
(Máscaras abismo)
nylon, stones, plastic

Dialogue: Goggles, 1968
(Diálogo: Óculos)
goggles, metal, mirrors, rubber

Goggles, 1968
(Óculos)
goggles, metal, mirrors, rubber

Sensorial Gloves, 1968
(Luvas sensoriais)
gloves, balls

Biological Architectures: Birth, 1969
(Arquiteturas biológicas: Nascimento)
plastic, net

Living Structures, 1969
(Estruturas vivas)
elastic

Straitjacket, 1969
(Camisa-de-força)
stones, nylon, elastic

Collective Body, 1970
(Corpo coletivo)
fabric

Cannibalism, 1973
(Canibalismo)
plastic, fruit

Tunnel, 1973
(Túnel)
cloth

Elastic Net, 1973
(Rede de elastico)
elastic

The World of Lygia Clark, 1973
(O mundo de Lygia Clark)
24-minute video

Rosácea, 1974–75
performance
cardboard, air, shells, plastic, string, fabric

Consulting Room, Relational Objects, 1978
(Consultório, Objetos relacionais)
bed, styrofoam beads, plastic, objects

Memory of the Body, 1985
(Memória do corpo)
28-minute video

Replicas commissioned in part by SITE Santa Fe.
   Originally shown in the Museo de Arte
   Moderna do Rio de Janeiro, Rio de Janeiro,
   Brazil
Courtesy of The Clark Family Collection

DILLER + SCOFIDIO

Room 120, 1999
audio-visual installation
Site-specific project produced by SITE Santa Fe
Courtesy of the artists

DR. GALENTIN GATEV

Motor Engines with a Regional Purpose,
   Evidence, 1998–99
installation with video projection,
   motorized sculpture
approximately 9 x 9 x 20 feet
Courtesy of the artist

GREENPEACE

Blood on the ice from seal cull, Newfoundland,
   Canada, 1981
photograph by Greenpeace/Gleizes
46 x 69 inches
Courtesy of Greenpeace International Photolibrary,
   Amsterdam, Netherlands

Action against Ark Royal, a British ship
   carrying nuclear weapons, Hamburg,
   Germany, 1989
photograph by Greenpeace/Venneman
46 x 69 inches
Courtesy of Greenpeace International Photolibrary,
   Amsterdam, Netherlands

End nuclear threats, placement of 5,000 crosses
   at Bohunice Nuclear Power Plant, Czech
   Republic, to commemorate the fifth
   anniversary of the accident at Chernobyl
   Power Plant, Ukraine, 1991
photograph by Greenpeace/Bindziarovo
46 x 69 inches
Courtesy of Greenpeace International Photolibrary,
   Amsterdam, Netherlands

*Action against Indian and Pakistani nuclear
   testing,* Taj Mahal, Agra, India, 1998
photograph by Greenpeace/Morgan
46 x 69 inches
Courtesy of Greenpeace International Photolibrary,
   Amsterdam, Netherlands

*Action against the nuclear-powered aircraft
   carrier U.S.S. Eisenhower,* Palma de Mallorca,
   Spain, 1998
photograph by Greenpeace/Gremo
15 x 17 feet
Courtesy of Greenpeace International Photolibrary,
   Amsterdam, Netherlands

Actions through the years, 1999
11-minute video
Courtesy of Greenpeace International Videolibrary,
   Amsterdam, Netherlands

YOLANDA GUTIÉRREZ

*The river whispers to us, and the snake
   hisses,* 1999
(Nos susurra el rio y silva la serpiente)
dried corn, twine, and plastic sculpture
approximately 82 feet long
Site-specific project produced by SITE Santa Fe
Courtesy of Espace d'Art Yvonamor Palix, Paris, France,
   and Mexico City, Mexico
With thanks to Centro Cultural Ixchel de Cozumel

MONA HATOUM

Map, 1998
installation with glass marbles
approximately 25 x 48 feet
Courtesy of the artist and Alexander and Bonin,
   New York, New York

CARL MICHAEL VON HAUSSWOLFF

Galisteo Dancehall Séance, 1999
audio-visual installation
variable dimensions

*Operation of Spirit Communication (New
   Mexico Basic Minimalism Séance),* 1999
audio installation
variable dimensions

Red Night, 1999
light installation
variable dimensions

All site-specific projects produced by SITE
   Santa Fe with support from the American-
   Scandinavian Foundation, New York,
   New York; and the Moderna Museet,
   Stockholm, Sweden
Courtesy of the artist and Andréhn-Schiptjenko Gallery,
   Stockholm, Sweden

CARSTEN HÖLLER

Sphere, 1998
(Kugel)
aluminum sculpture
approximately 7 feet in diameter
Courtesy of the artist and Museum für
   Gegenwartskunst, Basel, Switzerland

Crows and Lederhosen, 1999
(Krähen und lederhose)
installation with preserved crows
   and lederhosen
variable dimensions
Private collection, Milan, Italy

SIMONE AABERG KÆRN

Royal Greenland, 1995
10-minute video
Courtesy of the artist

wanna fly, 1995
video installation with 3 monitors and
    photographs
Courtesy of the artist

Camping in the clouds, 1999
participatory flight performance

ZWELETHU MTHETHWA

Some Sacred Homes, 1999
5 photographs on collaged newspapers
    and paint
50 x 63 inches each
Courtesy of the artist and Marco Noire Contemporary
    Art, Torino, Italy

NIKOS NAVRIDIS

Looking for a Place from the series
    The Question of the Age of the Void, 1999
19-minute, 30-second video installation,
    4 projections
With support from SITE Santa Fe; the
    Municipality of Athens, Greece; and Akto
    Art and Design School, Athens, Greece
Courtesy of the artist

SHIRIN NESHAT

Rapture, 1999
13-minute video installation, 2 projections
Courtesy of the artist; Patrick Painter, Inc., Santa
    Monica, California; and Barbara Gladstone Gallery,
    New York, New York

RIVANE NEUENSCHWANDER

Common Place, 1999
talcum powder swept on the floor
variable dimensions
Courtesy of the artist; Galeria Carmargo Vilaça,
    São Paulo, Brazil; and Stephen Friedman Gallery,
    London, England

GABRIEL OROZCO

From Dog Shit to Irma Vep, 1997
44-minute video
Courtesy of the artist and Marian Goodman Gallery,
    New York, New York

PIPILOTTI RIST

Looking for a Place (TV Program), 1999
30-minute video broadcast on Santa Fe
    Community Television, Channel 6
Courtesy of the artist; Luhring Augustine,
    New York, New York; and Galerie Hauser
    & Wirth, Zürich, Switzerland

FRANCISCO RUIZ DE INFANTE

Mixing the Air (Sabotage), 1999
    Zone 1: Place for Secret Activities
    Zone 2: Curiosity
    Zone 3: Control
    Zone 4: Learning
installations with infrared sensor, air, water,
    sound, light, and video projections
variable dimensions
Site-specific project produced by SITE Santa Fe
    with support from the Ministerio de Asuntos
    Exteriores, Madrid, Spain
Courtesy of the artist and Elba Benítez Galería,
    Madrid, Spain

BÜLENT ŞANGAR

Feast of Sacrifice, 1997–99
10 photographs
26 x 40 inches, 40 x 60 inches
Courtesy of the artist

ARSEN SAVADOV

Donbass-Chocolate, 1997
9 photographs, ballet tutus
photographs: 30 x 40 inches, 50 x 90 inches
Courtesy of the artist

ARSEN SAVADOV / GEORGY SENCHENKO

Welcome, 1996–99
text installation
Courtesy of the artists

Untitled, 1998
edition of 20,000 postcards for distribution
Courtesy of the artists

CHARLENE TETERS

Mound: To the Heroes, 1999
installation with sand, nylon, and photo mural
approximately 13 x 9 x 24 feet
Produced by Lannan Foundation, Santa Fe,
   New Mexico
Courtesy of the artist

Obelisk: To the Heroes, 1999
adobe obelisk embedded with donated objects
approximately 29 feet high
Site-specific project produced by Lannan
   Foundation, Santa Fe, New Mexico
Courtesy of the artist

SERGIO VEGA

Picnic: The Golden Age with Mosquitos, 1999
diorama with preserved wildlife, artificial
   fruit and plants, photographs, paintings,
   audio, and text
approximately 10 x 12 x 8 feet
Produced by SITE Santa Fe
Courtesy of the artist and Basilico Fine Arts, New York,
   New York

Telephones of Paradise, 1999
11 photographs and text panels
40 x 30 inches each
Courtesy of the artist and Basilico Fine Arts, New York,
   New York

MIWA YANAGI

Elevator Girl House 1F, 1997
2 photographs
94 x 78 inches each
Collection of the Kyoto Municipal Museum
   of Art, Kyoto, Japan
Courtesy of the artist

Eternal City 1, 1998
2 billboards
12 x 24 feet each
Courtesy of the artist and Yoshiko Isshiki, Tokyo, Japan

ARTISTS' BIOGRAPHIES

HELENA ALMEIDA

Born 1934, Lisbon, Portugal

Lives and works in Lisbon, Portugal

Selected Solo Exhibitions:

Centro Galego de Arte Contemporanea,
    Santiago de Compostela, Spain, 2000

Dentro de Mim, Galeria Presença,
    Porto, Portugal, 1998

Entrada Azul, Casa de America,
    Madrid, Spain, 1997

Selected Group Exhibitions:

Brazil 2000, Culturgest, Caixa Geral
    de Depósitos, Lisbon, Portugal, 2000

Circa 1968, Museu de Serralves,
    Porto, Portugal, 1999

*Ein Leuchtturm ist ein trauriger und
    glucklicher Ort*, Akademie der Kunste,
    Berlin, Germany, 1998

GHADA AMER

Born 1963, Cairo, Egypt

Lives and works in New York, New York

Selected Solo Exhibitions:

Deitch Projects, New York, New York, 2000

Brownstone, Corréard & Cie, Paris, France, 1999

Centro Andaluz de Arte Contemporáneo,
    Seville, Spain, 1999

Selected Group Exhibitions:

Whitney Biennial, Whitney Museum of
    American Art, New York, New York, 2000

Corps Social, École Nationale Supérieure
    des Beaux-Arts, Paris, France, 1999

48th International Venice Biennale, dAPERTutto,
    Venice, Italy, 1999

JANINE ANTONI

Born 1964, Freeport, Bahamas

Lives and works in New York, New York

Selected Solo Exhibitions:

imbed, Luhring Augustine, New York,
    New York, 1999

Swoon, Whitney Museum of American Art,
    New York, New York, 1998

Slip of the Tongue, Centre for Contemporary
    Arts, Glasgow, Scotland, 1995

Selected Group Exhibitions:

*The American Century: Art and Culture
    1950–2000*, Whitney Museum of
    American Art, New York, New York,
    1999–2000

*Regarding Beauty: A View of the Late Twentieth
    Century*, Hirshhorn Museum and Sculpture
    Garden, Washington, DC, 1999

*On Life, Beauty, Translations and Other
    Difficulties: 5th International Istanbul
    Biennial*, Istanbul, Turkey, 1997

MONICA BONVICINI

Born 1965, Venice, Italy

Lives and works in Berlin, Germany

Selected Solo Exhibitions:

RUN, TAKE one SQUARE or two, Kunstverein
    Salzburg, Salzburg, Austria, 2000

BEDTIMESQUARE, Galleria Emi Fontana, Milan,
    Italy, 1999

Mehdi Chouakri Gallery, Berlin, Germany, 1999

Selected Group Exhibitions:

Das Haus in der Kunst, Deichtorhalle Hamburg,
    Hamburg, Germany, 2000

Berlin Biennial, Berlin, Germany, 1999

48th International Venice Biennale, dAPERTutto,
    Venice, Italy, 1999

LOUISE BOURGEOIS

Born 1911, Paris, France
Lives and works in New York, New York

Selected Solo Exhibitions:

Louise Bourgeois: Inaugural Installation of the Tate Modern at Turbine Hall, Tate Modern, London, England, 2000

Louise Bourgeois: Architecture and Memory, Museo Nacional Centro de Arte Reina Sofía, Madrid, Spain, 1999–2000

capc Musée d'art contemporain, Bordeaux, France, 1998

Selected Group Exhibitions:

Close Encounters: New Art from Old, The National Gallery, London, England, 2000

The American Century: Art and Culture 1950–2000, Whitney Museum of American Art, New York, New York, 1999–2000

48th International Venice Biennale, dAPERTutto, Venice, Italy, 1999

TANIA BRUGUERA

Born 1968, Havana, Cuba
Lives and works in Havana, Cuba, and Chicago, Illinois

Selected Solo Exhibitions:

Vera van Laer Gallery, Antwerp, Belgium, 1999

El peso de la culpa, Tejadillo 214, Havana, Cuba, 1997

Cabeza Abajo, Espacio Aglutinador, Havana, Cuba, 1996

Selected Group Exhibitions:

Happening, Stedelijk Museum voor Actuele Kunst Gent, Ghent, Belgium, 1999

Maps of Desire, Kunsthalle Wien, Vienna, Austria, 1999

Videodrome, The New Museum of Contemporary Art, New York, New York, 1999

CAI GUO-QIANG

Born 1957, Quanzhou City, Fujian Province, China
Lives and works in New York, New York

Selected Solo Exhibitions:

Project for Projects, Fondation Cartier pour l'art contemporain, Paris, France, 2000

I am the Y2K Bug, Kunsthalle Wien, Vienna, Austria, 1999

No Construction, No Destruction: Bombing the Taiwan Museum of Art, Taiwan Museum of Art, Taichung, Taiwan, 1998

Selected Group Exhibitions:

48th International Venice Biennale, dAPERTutto, Venice, Italy, 1999

Wounds: Between Democracy and Redemption in Contemporary Art, Moderna Museet, Stockholm, Sweden, 1998

The Hugo Boss Prize, Guggenheim Museum SoHo, New York, New York, 1996

LYGIA CLARK

Born 1920, Belo Horizonte, Brazil
Died 1988, Rio de Janeiro, Brazil

Selected Solo Exhibitions:

Museu de Arte Moderna do Rio de Janeiro, Rio de Janeiro, Brazil, 1999–2000

Museu de Arte Moderna de São Paulo, São Paulo, Brazil, 1999

Fundação Serralves, Porto, Portugal, 1998

Selected Group Exhibitions:

Brasil 500 anos: XXV Bienal de São Paulo, São Paulo, Brazil, 2000

Documenta X, Kassel, Germany, 1997

Latin American Artists of the Twentieth Century, Museum of Modern Art, New York, New York, 1993

DILLER & SCOFIDIO

ELIZABETH DILLER
Born 1954, Lodz, Poland
Lives and works in New York, New York

RICARDO SCOFIDIO
Born 1935, New York, New York
Lives and works in New York, New York

Selected Projects:

The American Lawn: Surface of Everyday Life,
 Canadian Centre for Architecture, Montreal,
 Canada, 1999

EJM1 Man Walking at Ordinary Speed and
 EJM2: Inertia, two dance collaborations with
 the Lyon Ballet Opera and Charleroi Danses,
 Lyon, France, 1999

Jet Lag, a multimedia work for the stage, MASS
 MoCA, North Adams, Massachussetts, 1999

Master/Slave, Fondation Cartier pour l'art
 contemporain, Paris, France, 1999

Refresh, a web project for Dia Center for
 the Arts, New York, New York, 1999

InterClone Hotel, Atatürk Airport, *On Life,
 Beauty, Translations and Other Difficulties:
 5th International Biennial*, Istanbul,
 Turkey, 1997

DR. GALENTIN GATEV
Born 1960, Teteven, Bulgaria
Lives and works in Botevgrad, Bulgaria

Selected Solo Exhibitions:

Something Like an Old Blotter, Waszkowiak
 Gallery, Berlin, Germany, 1998

Corpus Alienum, Municipal Art Gallery, Sofia,
 Bulgaria, 1996

Only Possible Way (Gallery-Cause, Mine-Effect),
 Ata Ray Gallery, Sofia, Bulgaria, 1996

Selected Group Exhibitions:

Bulgariaavantgarde, Künstlerwerkstatt,
 Munich, Germany, 1998

Manifesta 2, Luxembourg City, Luxembourg,
 1998

Photo and Video Art from Bulgaria, ifa Gallery,
 Berlin, Germany, 1997

GREENPEACE
Founded 1971, Vancouver, Canada

Selected Actions:

*Cease climate change by promoting renewable
 energy sources*, protested against BP Amoco's
 plans for Arctic oil exploration and development, Artic Ocean, 2000

Protect the oceans, disrupted illegal Japanese
 whaling program, Southern Ocean Whale
 Sanctuary, Antarctic, 2000

Create a toxic-free environment, won emergency
 ban on vinyl toys in Europe, 1999

Stop genetic engineering, ignited debate over
 safety of genetically engineered foods in
 USA, 1999

Save the ancient forests, stopped shipment of
 newsprint made in part from ancient forests,
 Long Beach, California, 1998

End nuclear threats, placement of 5,000 crosses
 at Bohunice Nuclear Power Plant, Czech
 Republic, to commemorate the fifth
 anniversary of the accident at Chernobyl
 Power Plant, Ukraine, 1991

YOLANDA GUTIÉRREZ

Born 1970, Mexico City, Mexico
Lives and works in Cozumel, Mexico

Selected Solo Exhibitions:

Espace d'Art Yvonamor Palix, Paris,
  France, 1999
Galerie Nationale du Jeu de Paume, Paris,
  France, 1999
Tierra Virgen, Museo de Arte Carrillo Gil,
  Mexico City, Mexico, 1997

Selected Group Exhibitions:

Sous la grisaille de Mexico, Espace d'Art
  Yvonamor Palix, Paris, France 1999
La Corriente, Culturgest, Caixa Geral
  de Depósitos, Lisbon, Portugal, 1998
*On Life, Beauty, Translations and Other
  Difficulties: 5th International Istanbul
  Biennial*, Istanbul, Turkey, 1997

MONA HATOUM

Born 1952, Beirut, Lebanon
Lives and works in London, England

Selected Solo Exhibitions:

*Mona Hatoum: The Entire World as a Foreign
  Land*, Tate Britain, London, England, 2000
Museum of Contemporary Art, Chicago,
  Illinois, 1997
Musée national d'art moderne, Centre Georges
  Pompidou, Paris, France, 1994

Selected Group Exhibitions:

*The XXth Century: One Century of Art in
  Germany*, Neue Nationalgalerie, Berlin,
  Germany, 1999
*Wounds: Between Democracy and Redemption
  in Contemporary Art*, Moderna Museet,
  Stockholm, Sweden, 1998
46th Venice Biennale, Identity and Alterity,
  Venice, Italy, 1995

CARL MICHAEL VON HAUSSWOLFF

Born 1961, Linkoping, Sweden
Lives and works in Stockholm, Sweden

Selected Solo Exhibitions:

SŠUC Gallery, Ljubljana, Slovenia, 1999
Andréhn-Schiptjenko, Stockholm,
  Sweden, 1998
Kiasma Museum of Contemporary Art,
  Helsinki, Finland, 1998

Selected Group Exhibitions:

*Absolut: Los Angeles International Biennial
  Art Invitational*, Robert Berman Gallery,
  Los Angeles, California, 1999
Cities on the Move, Reno Hotel, Bangkok,
  Thailand, 1999
Young/Old, Wäinö Aaltonen Museum of Art,
  Turku, Finland, 1999

CARSTEN HÖLLER

Born 1961, Brussels, Belgium
Lives and works in Cologne, Germany

Selected Solo Exhibitions:

Sanatorium, Kunst-Werke, Berlin,
  Germany, 1999
New World, Museum für Gegenwartskunst,
  Basel, Switzerland, and Moderna Museet,
  Stockholm, Sweden, 1998–99
Glück, Kunstverein in Hamburg, Hamburg,
  Germany, 1996

Selected Group Exhibitions:

Présumés Innocents, capc Musée d'art
  contemporain, Bordeaux, France, 2000
Documenta X, Kassel, Germany, 1997
Manifesta 1, Rotterdam, The Netherlands, 1996

SIMONE AABERG KÆRN

Born 1969, Copenhagen, Denmark

Lives and works in Copenhagen, Denmark

Selected Solo Exhibitions:

Sisters in the Sky, Project Room, ARCO, Madrid,
Spain, 2000

Air, Kunstakademiets kunstforening,
Copenhagen, Denmark, 1995

wanna fly, SAGA Basement, Copenhagen,
Denmark, 1995

Selected Group Exhibitions:

48th International Venice Biennale, dAPERTutto,
Venice, Italy, 1999

Zeitwenden, Kunstmuseum Bonn, Rheinisches
Landesmuseum, and Stiftung für Kunst und
Kultur, Bonn, Germany, 1999

Nordic Nomads, White Columns, New York,
New York, 1998

ZWELETHU MTHETHWA

Born 1960, Durban, Kwazulu Natal, South Africa

Lives and works in Cape Town, South Africa

Selected Solo Exhibitions:

Gallery Jensen, Hamburg, Germany, 1999

Project Room, ARCO, Madrid, Spain, 1999

Marco Noire Contemporary Art,
San Sebastiano, Italy, 1998

Selected Group Exhibitions:

Göteborgs Konstmuseum, Göteborg,
Sweden, 1999

Africa by Africa, Barbican Art Gallery, London,
England, 1998

*Yesterday Begins Tomorrow: Ideals, Dreams,
and the Contemporary Awakening*, Center for
Curatorial Studies, Bard College, Annandale-
on-Hudson, New York, 1998

NIKOS NAVRIDIS

Born 1958, Athens, Greece

Lives and works in Athens, Greece

Selected Solo Exhibitions:

MUCA Gallery, Museo Universitario
Contemporáneo de Arte, Mexico City,
Mexico, 1999

Project Room, ARCO, Madrid, Spain, 1999

Epikentro Contemporary Art Center, Athens,
Greece, 1997

Selected Group Exhibitions:

Medialization, Edsvic Art Center, Stockholm,
Sweden, 1998

*On Life, Beauty, Translations and Other
Difficulties: 5th International Istanbul
Biennial*, Istanbul, Turkey, 1997

XXIII Bienal de São Paulo, São Paulo, Brazil,
1996

SHIRIN NESHAT

Born 1957, Qazvin, Iran

Lives and works in New York, New York

Selected Solo Exhibitions:

Serpentine Gallery, London, England, 2000

The Art Institute of Chicago, Chicago,
Illinois, 1999

The Tate Gallery, London, England, 1998

Selected Group Exhibitions:

Whitney Biennial, Whitney Museum of
American Art, New York, New York, 2000

Carnegie International 1999/2000, The Carnegie
Museum of Art, Pittsburgh, Pennsylvania,
1999–2000

48th International Venice Biennale, dAPERTutto,
Venice, Italy, 1999

RIVANE NEUENSCHWANDER

Born 1967, Belo Horizonte, Brazil
Lives and works in Belo Horizonte, Brazil

Selected Solo Exhibitions:

Galeria Camargo Vilaça, São Pāulo, Brazil, 2000

Syndrome, Iaspis Galleriet, Stockholm,
   Sweden, 2000

Stephen Friedman Gallery, London,
   England, 1999

Selected Group Exhibitions:

XXIV Bienal de São Paulo, São Paulo, Brazil, 1998

*Bili Bidjocka, Los Carpinteros, and Rivane
   Neuenschwander*, New Museum of
   Contemporary Art, New York, New York, 1998

*On Life, Beauty, Translations and Other
   Difficulties: 5th International Istanbul Biennial*,
   Istanbul, Turkey, 1997

GABRIEL OROZCO

Born 1962, Jalapa, Veracruz, Mexico
Lives and works in New York, New York

Selected Solo Exhibitions:

The Museum of Contemporary Art,
   Los Angeles, California, 2000

Museum Studies 5: Gabriel Orozco,
   Philadelphia Museum of Art, Philadelphia,
   Pennsylvania, 1999

Portikus Frankfurt am Main, Frankfurt,
   Germany, 1999

Selected Group Exhibitions:

*Orbis Terrarum: Worldmaking, Cartography,
   and Contemporary Art: Antwerpen Open*,
   Antwerpen, Germany, 2000

Carnegie International 1999/2000, The Carnegie
   Museum of Art, Pittsburgh, Pennsylvania,
   1999–2000

PIPILOTTI RIST

Born 1962, Rheintal, Switzerland
Lives and works in Zürich, Switzerland

Selected Solo Exhibitions:

Remake of the Weekend (french), Musée
   d'art moderne de la ville de Paris, Paris,
   France, 1999

Remake of the Weekend à la zurichoise,
   Kunsthalle Zürich, Zürich, Switzerland, 1999

Wadsworth Atheneum, Hartford,
   Connecticut, 1998

Selected Group Exhibitions:

The Hugo Boss Prize, Guggenheim Museum
   SoHo, New York, New York, 1998

Luhring Augustine, New York, New York, 1998

Unmapping the Earth: Kwangju Biennale,
   Kwangju, South Korea, 1997

FRANCISCO RUIZ DE INFANTE

Born 1966, Vitoria-Gasteiz, Spain
Lives and works in Paris, France

Selected Solo Exhibitions:

Room of Languages, Museo Nacional Centro
   de Arte Reina Sofía, Madrid, Spain, 1998

Flight Simulators, Ujazdowski Castle, Warsaw,
   Poland, 1998

Survival Sounds, La Ferme de Buisson, Paris,
   France, 1997

Selected Group Exhibitions:

*The Tower Wounded by Lightning:
   The Impossible as an Aim*, Guggenheim
   Museum Bilbao, Bilbao, Spain, 2000

Banc d'essais nº2, Centre Santa Mònica,
   Barcelona, Spain, 1998

15th World Wide Video Exhibition, Stedelijk
   Museum, Amsterdam, The Netherlands, 1997

BÜLENT ŞANGAR

Born 1965, Eskişehir, Turkey
Lives and works in Istanbul, Turkey

Selected Solo Exhibitons:
Project Room, ARCO, Madrid, Spain, 2000
Artoteek Den Haag, The Hague,
  The Netherlands, 1999
Urart Art Gallery, Istanbul, Turkey, 1995

Selected Group Exhibitions:
Borderline Syndrome—Energies of Defence:
  Manifesta 3, Ljubljana, Slovenia, 2000
Man + Space, Kwangju Biennial, Kwangju,
  Korea, 2000
XXIV Bienal de São Paulo, São Paulo,
  Brazil, 1998

ARSEN SAVADOV /
GEORGY SENCHENKO

ARSEN SAVADOV

Born 1962, Kiev, Ukraine
Lives and works in Kiev, Ukraine

GEORGY SENCHENKO

Born 1962, Kiev, Ukraine
Lives and works in Kiev, Ukraine

Selected Exhibitions:
Deepinsider, Guelman Gallery, Moscow,
  Russia, 1998
The Works of Savadov & Senchenko,
  Berman Gallery, New York, New York, 1992
Central Artist House, Moscow, Russia, 1991

Selected Group Exhibitions:
After the Wall, Moderna Museet, Stockholm,
  Sweden, 1999
White Dresses, Center for Curatorial Studies,
  Bard College, Annandale-on-Hudson,
  New York, 1998
Manifesta 1, Rotterdam, The Netherlands, 1996

CHARLENE TETERS

Born 1952, Spokane, Washington
Lives and works in Santa Fe, New Mexico

Selected Solo Exhibitions:
Route 66 Revisited: It Was Only An Indian,
  516 ¡Magnifico! Artspace, Albuquerque,
  New Mexico, 2000
We, The Invisible People, Cheney Cowles
  Museum, Spokane, Washington, 1996
It Was Only An Indian, American Indian
  Community House Gallery, New York,
  New York, 1995

Selected Group Exhibitions:
Monothon 13, The College of Santa Fe and SITE
  Santa Fe, Santa Fe, New Mexico, 1998
The Rio Grande Project: A River Thirsting For
  Itself, Santa Fe Council for the Arts and
  The College of Santa Fe, Santa Fe,
  New Mexico, 1997
Visiting Artist Exhibition, Ohio State University,
  Columbus, Ohio, 1995

SERGIO VEGA

Born 1959, Buenos Aires, Argentina
Lives and works in New York, New York

Selected Solo Exhibitions:
Excerpts from El Paraíso en el Nuevo Mundo,
  Basilico Fine Arts, New York, New York, 1999
Espacio 204, Caracas, Venezuela, 1997
Memoirs of an Outspoken Parrot, Basilico Fine
  Arts, New York, New York, 1996

Selected Group Exhibitions:
Amnesia, Christopher Grimes Gallery and Track
  16 Gallery, Santa Monica, California, 1998
The Garden of Forking Paths, Kunstforeningen,
  Copenhagen, Denmark, 1998
Trade Routes: History and Geography: 2nd
  Johannesburg Biennale, Johannesburg, South
  Africa, 1997

MIWA YANAGI

Born 1967, Kobe City, Japan
Lives and works in Kyoto, Japan

Selected Solo Exhibitions:

Gallery KODAMA, Osaka, Japan, 1999
Art Space Niji, Kyoto, Japan, 1998
Criterium 31, Contemporary Art Gallery,
   Art Tower Mito, Ibaragi, Japan, 1997

Selected Group Exhibitions:

Signs of Life: Melbourne International Biennial,
   Melbourne, Australia, 1999
Site of Desire: Taipei Biennial, Taipei City
   Museum of Contemporary Art, Taipei,
   Taiwan, 1998
PROSPECT '96, Schirn Kunsthalle Frankfurt,
   Frankfurt, Germany, 1996

ACKNOWLEDGMENTS

The exhibition *Looking for a Place* and this catalogue would not have been made possible without the generous support of the following corporations, foundations, organizations, and individuals:

Major Contributors

Anonymous

The Board of Directors of SITE Santa Fe

The Brown Foundation, Inc., Houston

The Burnett Foundation

The Jodi Carson Memorial Fund

The Dunlevy-Milbank Foundation, Inc.

Agnes Gund and Daniel Shapiro

James Kelly Contemporary / SITE Unseen
  Benefit Art Sale

Lannan Foundation

LLWW Foundation

McCune Charitable Foundation

The Rockefeller Foundation

Sotheby's and Sotheby's International Realty

Additional Contributors

Gay Block and Rabbi Malka Drucker

Madelin Coit and Alan Levin

Natalie and F. Gregory Fitz-Gerald

Bobbie Foshay-Miller and Chuck Miller

Elizabeth Glassman

Anne and Graham Jones

Jeanne and Michael L. Klein

Emily Fisher Landau and Sheldon Landau

Nancy and Dr. Robert C. Magoon

Anne and John L. Marion

Susan and Lawrence Marx

Marlene Meyerson

Caroline and Martin Proyect

Eliza Lovett Randall

Louisa Stude Sarofim

Marcia Southwick and Dr. Murray Gell-Mann

Donna and Howard Stone

Akto Art and Design School, Athens, Greece

The American-Scandinavian Foundation,
  New York, New York

Appelbaum-Kahn Foundation, Malibu,
  California

The British Council, Washington, D.C.

City of Santa Fe Arts Commission and the 1%
  Lodger's Tax, Santa Fe, New Mexico

Cultural Services of the French Embassy,
  New York, New York

Danish Contemporary Art Foundation,
  Copenhagen, Denmark

Instituto de Arte Contemporânea, Lisbon,
  Portugal

Italian Cultural Institute, Los Angeles,
  California

Toby D. Lewis Philanthropic Fund, Cleveland,
  Ohio

Ministerio de Asuntos Exteriores, Madrid,
  Spain

Mittler Family Foundation, Inc., South Bend,
  Indiana

Moderna Museet, Stockholm, Sweden

Municipality of Athens, Greece

Philip Morris Companies Inc., New York,
  New York

In-Kind Contributors

Art Foundry, Inc, Santa Fe, New Mexico

Art Now Gallery Guide, Clinton, New Jersey

Arté, Santa Fe, New Mexico

Frieda and Jim Arth

Bohemia Beer, San Ysidro, California

Cookworks, Santa Fe, New Mexico

Linda Durham Contemporary, Galisteo,
    New Mexico

John Hart Fine Wine Ltd., Santa Fe,
    New Mexico

Ann Kippen and Louis Grachos

Los Alamos Airport, Los Alamos, New Mexico

Lumber, Inc., Santa Fe, New Mexico

Balene McCormick

Alicia and William A. Miller

New Mexico State Capitol Art Foundation,
    Santa Fe, New Mexico

Ohori's Coffee Tea & Chocolate, Santa Fe,
    New Mexico

Our Lady of Guadalupe Parish, Santa Fe,
    New Mexico

Paseo Pottery, Santa Fe, New Mexico

Plan B Evolving Arts, Santa Fe, New Mexico

Public Services of New Mexico, Inc., Santa Fe,
    New Mexico

Rodeo Electrical Services, Inc., Santa Fe,
    New Mexico

Sam's Construction Co., Santa Fe, New Mexico

San Ildefonso Pueblo, New Mexico

Santa Fe Budget Inn, Santa Fe, New Mexico

Santa Fe Community Television, Santa Fe,
    New Mexico

Santa Fe Shine, Santa Fe, New Mexico

Santa Fe Southern Railway Station, Santa Fe,
    New Mexico

Dede and Henry Schuhmacher

Sociedad de San José de Galisteo /
    Cornerstones, Galisteo, New Mexico

Wholesale Building Supply, Santa Fe,
    New Mexico

Supporters and Lenders

Alexander and Bonin, New York, New York

Basilico Fine Arts, New York, New York

Elba Benítez Galería, Madrid, Spain

Galeria Camargo Vilaça, São Paulo, Brazil

Galleria Massimo de Carlo, Milan, Italy

Cheim & Read, New York, New York

Mehdi Chouakri Gallery, Berlin, Germany

The Clark Family Collection, Rio de Janeiro,
    Brazil

D'Amelio-Terras Gallery, New York, New York

Deitch Projects, New York, New York

Epikentro Contemporary Art Center, Athens,
    Greece

Espace d'Art Yvonamor Palix, Paris, France,
    and Mexico City, Mexico

Galleria Emi Fontana, Milan, Italy

Barbara Gladstone Gallery, New York, New York

Marian Goodman Gallery, New York, New York

Galerie Hauser & Wirth, Zürich, Switzerland

Kyoto Municipal Museum of Art, Kyoto, Japan

Luhring Augustine, New York, New York

Luso-American Development Foundation
    Collection, Lisbon, Portugal

Museo de Arte Contemporâneo Mario Abreu,
    Maracay, Venezuela

Museu de Arte Moderna do Rio de Janeiro,
    Rio de Janeiro, Brazil

Museum für Gegenwartskunst, Basel,
    Switzerland

Marco Noire Contemporary Art, Torino, Italy

Patrick Painter, Inc., Santa Monica, California

Yoshiko Isshiki, Tokyo, Japan

SITE Santa Fe Staff

Louis Grachos
Director & Curator

Emily Alsen
Visitor Services Coordinator

Craig Anderson
Exhibitions Administrator

Kimberly A. Botza
Director's Assistant

Christina Cassidy
Public Relations

Marianne Dell
*Public Relations Assistant &
Publications Distribution*

Melissa Dubbin
*Registrar & Exhibitions
Assistant*

Dennis Esquivel
Facilities Assistant

Rebecca Friedman
Editor & Grant Writer

Margaret Grant
*Membership, Marketing &
Special Events*

Sarah S. King
*Catalogue Editor &
Special Projects*

Ann Kippen
Accounting Manager

Chris Nail
Education Coordinator

Judith Podmore
Head of Public Programming

Carey Schaefer
Administrative Assistant

Erin Shirreff
*Curatorial Assistant, Registrar
& Design*

Siobhan Spain
Office Administrator

Jill Treadwell
Administrative Assistant

Vivi Valentine
Administrative Assistant

Bryan Walker
*Administrative & Special
Events Assistant*

Interns
Travis Anderson
Jo Baker
Liz Batkin
Amelia Bauer
Maryt Fredrickson
Patrick Fredrickson
Laurel Gitlen
Savannah Gorton
Gretchen Ladd
Amanda Lechner
Perry Lowe
Turner Mark-Jacobs
Keli Mashburn
Ross McLain
Caitlin Parker
Karen Phillips
Wood Roberdeau
Alison Silverstein
Robin Waldman

Preparators
Carlos Beuth
Krysten Cunningham
Pam Ellison
Steve Fowler
Nathan Freeman
Sharon Gurnack
James Holmes
Rhonda Paynter
Terri Rolland
David Servoss
Peter Sprunt
David Teske
Tom Tiegler
Colin Zaug

Docents
Madelin Coit
Kathryn Davis
Dinah Guimaraens
Bill Hinsvark
Nancy Kriebel
Nick Livaich
Donald Meyer
Sally Mittler
Margaret Norcross
Eleanor Rappe
Celia Rumsey
Jennifer Schlesinger
Ginna Sloane
Rusty Spicer
Signe Stuart
Sarah Tyson
Peter Wiedmann
Judy Youens

Curator's Acknowledgments

Arakis	Okwui Enwezor	Geeta Kapur	Patrizia Sandretto Re
Art Forum Berlin	Fulya Erdemci	Udo Kittelmann	Rebaudengo
Félix de Azúa	Karim Francis	Julia Kristeva	Harald Szeemann
Alba Baeza	Rosina Gómez-Baeza	Werner Krüger	Jordi Terré
Emre Baykal	José Angel González	Llilian Llanes	Bilge Ugurlar
Francesco Bonami	Katerina Gregos	Ivo Mesquita	Young Chul Lee
Dan Cameron	Pepito Grillo	John Miller	Antonio Zaya
Isabel Carlos	Hou Hanru	Viktor Misiano	Octavio Zaya
Paolo Colombo	Yuko Hasegawa	Hans Ulrich Obrist	
María de Corral	Paulo Herkenhoff	Paul O'Reilly	
Sheila Deegan	Maaretta Jaukkuri	Adriano Pedrosa	

Director's Acknowledgments

The director would like to reiterate his gratitude for the extraordinary participation required by the scale of this exhibition to SITE Santa Fe's Board of Directors, staff, exhibition preparators, volunteers, and interns, as well as to those listed below:

Michael Anaya	Zane Fischer	Antonio López	Mary Royal
Robert Anaya	Tina Flores	Owen Lopez	Robert Saar
Frieda and Jim Arth	Bobbie Foshay-Miller and	Ruth Lopez	Cynthia Sanchez
Penelope Arth	Chuck Miller	Herbert Lotz	Father Michael Shea
Stuart Ashman	Stephanie French	Anne and John L. Marion	Sonic Youth
Boukman Eksperyans	Rebecca Friedman	Sam Martinez	Eugene Thaw
Steve Brugger	Agnes Gund and Daniel	Kathleen Merrill	Janet Voorhees
Sandy and Dr. Richard	Shapiro	Don Messic	Pam Walker
Carson	Susan Herter	Vesna Mladenovik	Laura Wilson
Linda Durham Contemporary	Bruce Hudspeth	Larry Ogan	Tomás Ybarra-Frausto
Richard Ellis	James Kelly	Richard Oldenburg	Peter Zavadil
Susan Emerling	Sarah King	Cornelia Providoli	
Jennifer Esperanza	Emily Fisher Landau	Paul Rainbird	
Susan Firestone	J. Patrick Lannan	Katherine Ross	

Photo Credits

Courtesy of Akto Art and Design School, Athens, Greece, pp. 78–79
Amelia Bauer, p. 74 (top)
Peter Bellamy, courtesy of Cheim & Read, New York, New York, p. 42
Cai Guo-Qiang, p. 47 (bottom)
Courtesy of Mehdi Chouakri Gallery, Berlin, Germany; and Galleria Emi Fontana, Milan Italy, pp. 40 (bottom), 41
Melissa Dubbin, p. 18
Jennifer Esperanza, cover
Laurel Gitlen, pp. 10–11
Courtesy of Galerie Hauser & Wirth, Zürich, Switzerland, pp. 88–89
Courtesy of Marian Goodman Gallery, New York, New York; and The Stedelijk Museum of Modern Art, Amsterdam, Netherlands, pp. 86–87

Greenpeace/Bindziarovo, courtesy of Greenpeace International Photolibrary, Amsterdam, Netherlands, p. 56
Greenpeace/Gleizes, courtesy of Greenpeace International Photolibrary, Amsterdam, Netherlands, p. 57
Greenpeace/Gremo, courtesy of Greenpeace International Photolibrary, Amsterdam, Netherlands, pp. 2–3
Courtesy of the Kyoto Municipal Museum of Art, Kyoto, Japan, pp. 108–109
Larry Lamay, courtesy of Luhring Augustine, New York, New York, pp. 38–39
Herbert Lotz, pp. 36 (top), 37, 40 (top), 44–45, 47 (top), 48–49, 51 (top), 52 (top), 53, 54 (top), 58–71, 74 (bottom), 76–77, 84, 90–93, 97, 98, 101–107, 110–111

Courtesy of the Luso-American Development Foundation Collection, Lisbon, Portugal, pp. 34–35
Courtesy of the Museum of New Mexico, Santa Fe, New Mexico, p. 16
Chris Nail, pp. 14–15, 24–25, 26, 32–33, 50, 51 (center and bottom), 52 (bottom), 55 (top), 85
Courtesy of Patrick Painter, Inc., Santa Monica, California; and Barbara Gladstone Gallery, New York, New York, pp. 80–81, 82–83
T. Harmon Parkhurst, courtesy of the Museum of New Mexico, Santa Fe, New Mexico pp. 6–7
Quesada/Burke, p. 43
Bill Jack Rodgers, courtesy of the Museum of New Mexico, Santa Fe, New Mexico, pp. 12–13
Joshua Willis, pp. 8–9